SCREEN LOVERS

SCREEN LOVERS

ANNE BILLSON
FOREWORD BY STEWART GRANGER

PHOTOGRAPHS FROM
THE KOBAL COLLECTION

ST. MARTIN'S PRESS
New York

First published in 1988 by
Conran Octopus Limited
37 Shelton Street
London WC2H 9HN

First U.S. Edition
10 9 8 7 6 5 4 3 2 1

Art Editor Ruth Prentice
Designer Pam Drewitt Smith
House Editor Joanna Bradshaw
Editor Mary Davies
Editorial Assistant Simon Willis
Production Michel Blake

Special thanks to Toni Lopopolo and Dave Kent

Library of Congress Cataloguing-in-Publication Data
Billson, Anne.
  Screen Lovers.
  1. Love in motion pictures. I. Title
PN1995.9.L6B5 1988   791.43'09'09354 88-15843
ISBN 0-312-02073-2

ISBN 0 312 020 732

Typeset by MS Filmsetting Limited
Printed in Shekou, China

Acknowledgments:
The publishers would like to thank the following film
distribution and production companies whose publicity film stills appear in this
book: Algi/Emelka, American International Pictures, André Paulvé, Argos, Batjac,
British Lion, Cannon, Cinéguild, CIP, Cocinor, Columbia, DeLaurentiis, Embassy,
First National, Gainsborough, Gaumont, Handmade Films, ICI, Landau/Park, Les
Films du Carosse/TFI, Les Films Marceau, London Films, Merchant-Ivory, MGM,
Nouvelles Editions, NSWFC, Ossard/Beneix Productions, Orion, Palomar/Associates
and Aldrich, Paramount, Paris/Juno Films, Pax Films, Phototeque, Ponti,
Productions Artistes Associés, Rank, RKO, Alexander and Ilya Salkind, Selznick
International, Seven Arts, SNC, Svensk Filmindustri, Touchstone/Buena Vista,
Twentieth Century-Fox, United Artists, Universal, Warner Bros.

Frontispiece: Rita Hayworth and Glenn Ford in *Gilda* (1946)

CONTENTS

FOREWORD
BY STEWART GRANGER

My mother was a film fan. She also suffered from claustrophobia, and because my father was an army officer and not interested in the cinema in any way, I was chosen to accompany her to the cinema from about the age of seven.

I remember us always searching in the dark for seats next to the aisle, so that she could make a quick getaway if her claustrophobia became too overpowering. Sitting excitedly next to her with my eyes glued to the flickering screen, I always dreaded being dragged out in the middle of some thrilling action scene. In those days the screens were bigger – much bigger – especially to a boy of seven. Scenes like the chariot race in *Ben Hur* (1926), or Douglas Fairbanks fighting off fifty pirates and storming the Bastille in *Scaramouche* (1923). On the other hand, if there was a love scene taking place on screen I didn't need much persuading to leave. In fact, it was a welcome relief. To most small boys, kissing scenes were an embarrassment, a bore, somehow slightly disgusting – and that was in the Twenties, when love scenes were extremely chaste. In the old days, a great deal was left to the imagination, which can be a very erotic sense, whereas now nothing is held back, and to my mind present-day love scenes are not in any way erotic, merely physical and animalistic. When will film-makers realise that copulation – though very pleasurable, if my memory serves me well – is not very pretty to watch, especially in close-up, with the accompanying gasps and groans. Embarrassing as hell.

As I grew older, however, the on-screen love scenes became slightly less offensive and I remember watching with pleasure as the handsome star Ramon Navarro kissed the adorable Alice Terry in *Scaramouche*. They were such a beautiful couple and their kiss so tender that it was hardly offensive at all to a nine year old, though little did I guess that I would one day play the Navarro role myself for MGM and get to kiss two leading ladies. I also enjoyed watching my hero Rudolph Valentino kiss the same lady in *The Four Horsemen of the Apocalypse,* although I did think he went a bit far in *The Sheik*. In *The Son of the Sheik* I didn't understand what was going

Phyllis Calvert and Stewart Granger in The Magic Bow (1947)
'We love each other – nothing else matters.' Stewart Granger, as the violinist Paganini, expresses one of the Screen Lover's abiding sentiments.

on, as Valentino's co-star, Agnes Ayres, always seemed to be fainting after he kissed her. Interesting! I wondered what his technique was, but I never discovered it myself. Try as I might over the years, not one of my lady friends or co-stars fainted when I kissed them, or when I did anything else to them, for that matter!

My first passionate on-screen kiss was in my first starring role in 1943. I had just come out of the army, and after appearing in a play with that marvellous actor Robert Donat, I was lucky enough to land the part of the hero in *The Man in Grey*, in which James Mason played the title role. I don't think the leading lady was overly enamoured of me, or me of her, yet we made three films together, all of which included passionate love scenes. I soon realised how horribly difficult it was to play love scenes with someone you didn't even like!

One evening, during World War II, exhausted after a day's 'romantic' filming at the studio and a nerve-wracking drive home through bomb-scarred London, I was already worrying about a passionate love scene at eight o'clock the following morning by the time I reached the front door. 'I can't do it!' I told my wife. But she assured me I'd be all right, and as she handed me a precious rationed drink she was no doubt secretly rather pleased that I was dreading playing a love scene with such a truly beautiful woman.

I did it, of course, but it wasn't easy. You can 'fake' on stage, but not in front of a camera; it has a most searching eye, which picks up everything. Somehow, you have to make yourself believe

Jean Simmons and Stewart Granger in Young Bess (1953)
A real-life husband and wife team as a pair of historical Screen Lovers. The Princess Elizabeth (soon to become Queen Elizabeth I of England) and her dashing navy sweetheart, Tom. Not many people have heard of Tom.

8

that you love and desire the lady in your arms; that she really turns you on. All this in front of a film crew of seventy or more rather uninterested onlookers, and, to make matters worse, often first thing in the morning.

I recall reading that Greta Garbo and John Gilbert, before acting a love scene, used to sip champagne, with violins playing offscreen to get them in the mood. Of course those were the silent films. In my day there was none of that. Usually there was an irate production manager on the set urging us to 'get the bloody scene right', and to 'stop messing up her hair — we're behind schedule'. We were always behind schedule. You'd think grabbing a woman and kissing her would be easy, but not at all. You'd be so busy trying to get the positioning right so as not to cover the lady's eyes or nose or cheekbone that you'd forget the make-up and smudge her lipstick or dislodge her eyelashes! And if you remembered the make-up, you forgot the hair — which was even worse. During love scenes, I had a tendency when leading up to 'the kiss' to grasp the lady by the back of the head, to be sure her mouth would be where I wanted it and I wouldn't slide into it and smudge the lipstick. But I had forgotten the hair and an hour's rearranging would follow — not at all popular with production. Today the messier the hair becomes, the more realistic, and quite right too. But in my day love scenes always had to be 'pretty'.

There is also the personal side of love scenes. I made a great many 'costume' films and of course, because of the budget, you usually only had one of each costume, so at night they were rushed out to the dry cleaners. In costume you perspire a lot, and after a few cleanings, when they heat up under the lights these costumes take on a personality that is extremely odiferous and not very romantic! I had a phobia, too, about bad breath and was constantly using a mouthwash and a throat spray, as well as deodorants on other parts of my body. Not so with all my leading ladies, and especially those who liked garlic! This is written from the actor's point of view, but actresses have to put up with the same handicaps.

A number of films include passionate love scenes when the lady sobs in your arms. One of my leading ladies especially loved to cry: she could bring floods of tears to her eyes at the drop of a hat. This did not mean that she was a great dramatic actress, but she did have a good control over her tear ducts. There was one drawback, though: when she cried her nose ran and it is not easy to kiss a lady passionately who has a very runny nose. I mean the mouth is very close to the nostrils — ugh! Maybe it's just me, perhaps I'm too sensitive.

But of one thing I'm absolutely sure: I couldn't have played love scenes the way they are played today, and I don't think any of the leading romantic actors of my day could have either, with the possible exception of my old chum Errol Flynn. Can you imagine Jimmy Stewart stripping off and diving in? Or Gary Cooper and Ronald Colman? Do you really think 'Duke' Wayne would have had any part of it? Mind you, the 'Duke' wasn't into kissing at all — he just hugged them to death! As for me, I just don't know how today's leading men can casually strip off and roll around with a nearly nude actress faking orgasms. I starred in some fifty films, most of which were romantic and included what we called passionate love scenes. My co-stars were such fantastically beautiful ladies as Rita Hayworth, Grace Kelly, Ava Gardner, Elizabeth Taylor, Jean Simmons and Deborah Kerr yet never once did my hands stray to any intimate parts of their anatomy! Today it's grab, grope, nibble and lick, and I suppose if I were fifty years younger I might think it was all part of a day's work. But I strongly doubt it. If there is another life — please God — don't make me a romantic actor; make me a heavy. Much more fun!

INTRODUCTION

In 1896, May Irwin and John C. Rice put their lips together and made cinema history. They were not the most glamorous of couples, and the film in question, Edison's *The Kiss*, lasted for less than a minute, leaving no time for such niceties as plot and character development. But the Screen Lover was born.

Motion-picture technology captured what hitherto had been a private act and exposed it, much magnified, to public scrutiny. Voyeurism would never be the same again: it had been legitimized as a mass spectacle, as something to be savoured and shared by hundreds of people sitting together in the dark. In the years that followed, those first flickering sideshows evolved into a full-blown storytelling industry; not only could audiences *watch* Screen Lovers being put through their intimate paces, they could also empathize with the emotions on display. 'Moving pictures' moved in both senses of the word.

There is more to the cinema than cinematography. Movies can induce laughter and tears, terror and awe. No matter how spectacular or outlandish a film's content, if we can relate to some core of emotional truth the springboard is clear for any flight of fantasy. We might not all have been monarchs or murderers, saints or sinners, but we all have some experience of life's basic emotions. Movies, when they succeed in weaving their magic spell, do so by drawing on a fund of feelings that are common to us all. Big budgets, interesting concepts and unusual camera angles are not in themselves enough to hold our attention for long; if the production values mask an emotional void, or if the film-maker's ideas cannot be expressed so that we can relate to them, the result will be tedium, pretentiousness and lousy box-office returns. The best stories are not just action; they are also *reaction*.

Interior monologue and first-person narrative might provide the basis for many a novel, but in the cinema, where emotions are concerned, it takes two to make a love story. There *are* movies with a cast of one, but not many. The essential element is the development of some sort of relationship. And in nearly every case it is the emotional relationship between male and female,

▲ May Irwin and John C. Rice in The Kiss (1896)

◄ Laraine Day and Robert Mitchum in The Locket (1946)
The man with 'bedroom eyes'.

because it is that which is perceived to strike a universal chord. Homosexual relationships, when they are not being treated as aberrations by film-makers, are depicted as variations on the universal standard.

The cinema has elevated love to the status of a religion, as both a refuge from life and a reason for living; a belief in love, like belief in the existence of a god, can give form and meaning to the senselessness of human existence. Friendship, parental feelings and patriotism all have their places in the cinematic canon, but it is love between men and women that is the most durable theme. Love is at once the most mysterious and most easily recognizable of emotions, and it is its very ambiguity which gives it infinite flexibility as a theme. 'Love' is a convenient catch-all term because love is really a combination of any number of other emotions: affection, familiarity, dependence, greed, lust, jealousy, fear and loathing. Love is shorthand for the entire range of human emotion, and Screen Lovers can run the proverbial gamut: they can strike passionate sparks off each other, or they can trade quips, or sashay, or sing in harmony, or spit poison. But there is always an emotional rapport of some kind.

Screen Lovers are not confined to the romantic film, though the great classics of the genre – *Camille* (1936), *Gone With the Wind* (1939), *Casablanca* (1942) – do provide us with some of their most memorable incarnations. Nor are Screen Lovers restricted to the realm of women's pictures, where the female characters, played by the likes of Bette Davis, Joan Crawford or Barbara Stanwyck, wallow magnificently in affairs of the heart and home. No, Screen Lovers have infiltrated every single genre that cinema has to offer (with the possible exception of the documentary), adapting like chameleons to their environments.

There can be few examples of the comedy which do not base at least part of their humour on the perceived differences between the sexes: on Margaret Dumont's stoic incomprehension in the face of Groucho's innuendo, for instance, or on the Walls of Jericho that go up between Clark Gable and Claudette Colbert in *It Happened One Night* (1934). In the musical, romance is the mainspring for both lyrics and choreography: every Fred must have his Ginger, and every brother must have his bride. If they're in love, then nothing on earth will prevent them from belting out a song on the subject, and a well-turned Carioca can be every bit as stimulating as the passionate clinch: it's all in the timing.

In the thriller, it is sexual obsession which embroils Fred MacMurray's *Double Indemnity* (1944) salesman in Barbara Stanwyck's murderous coils, or which propels any number of *film noir* characters towards the Mexican border, intrigue and death. In the epic, love can start wars and tear empires apart, or it can represent the personal happiness that must be sacrificed for king, country and civilization. Love interest can lighten the worthy load of the social drama or give warmth to the remote existences of great men and women: where would Lord Nelson be without Lady Hamilton, or Napoleon without Josephine? (Winning battles, no doubt, but with their human faces lost in the mists of history.) Horror and science fiction films often turn out to be love stories in disguise: *King Kong* (1933) and *Creature From the Black Lagoon* (1954) are no more immune to the attractions of the fair sex than the regular redblooded hero.

In the western or the war film, Screen Lovers are less frequently central to the main business of riding hard, living rough and shooting straight, but such relationships exist nonetheless as a reminder to the cowboy or soldier that there is something at home worth fighting for.

The cinema, in its passionate espousal of love and romance as a major theme, has always reflected shifting social attitudes in the real world. But, like all love affairs, it has been a two-way relationship. Movies, taking their cue from a reality that is itself feeding on a constant output of screen dreams, have become enmeshed in a mythology of their own making, and the mythology continues to colour our lives in a never-ending chain reaction. The twentieth-century concept of romance has been fed by decades of screen liaisons consummated in soft-focus close-up to the accompaniment of a suitably evocative soundtrack: lush strings, soaring chorals or Rachmaninoff's Piano Concerto Number 2.

The Screen Lovers have done our groundwork for us by sketching in all the shades of meaning between key phrases. *He* says: 'Here's looking at you, kid', to which *she* replies: 'Don't ask for the moon when we have the stars.' As Jack Lemmon says of Tony Curtis's Cary Grant

Greta Garbo and Gavin Gordon in Romance (1930)
In flagrante, watched by director Clarence Brown and cinematographer Williams Daniels.

impersonation in *Some Like It Hot* (1959): '*Nobody* talks like that.' But we do now, or, at least, we try to. Our most intimate conversations are peppered with oblique references and quotations which cloak our self-consciousness. The cinema has helped shape our perceptions and expectations of life and love. What woman could fail to be disappointed by real life when her ideal mate is an amalgam of Cary Grant, Robert Mitchum and Sean Connery? Even Grant had trouble coming to terms with his screen persona: 'Everyone wants to be Cary Grant,' he once said. '*I* want to be Cary Grant.' And what man will ever be able to find the woman who is Rita Hayworth, Sophia Loren *and* Brigitte Bardot, when even Hayworth admitted that every man she knew had 'fallen in love with Gilda and wakened with me'? If even the greatest of screen gods and goddesses found it impossible to live up to their own perfect screen images, what hope is there for us lesser mortals?

Where there is love, of course, there also lurks sex, and the cinema has helped to blur the boundary between the two. The Love Goddesses of the screen – Hayworth, Monroe, Bardot – were, in truth, Sex Goddesses. They presented an image of woman as something to be worshipped or desired, as idealized objects distinct from the reality of domestic life and shared responsibility: there never *was* a woman like Gilda, and you'd certainly never catch her doing the dishes. Reality rarely sells films; nor does it feed the public appetite for dreams. Screen Lovers have at least one of their feet set firmly in fantasy land, where no-one has to worry about the mortgage, where the housework does itself and where the love affair can take centre stage, unencumbered by mundane concerns.

Until the Sixties, film-makers were forced by censorship and public opinion to deal with sex through a combination of suggestion and symbolism which, by its appeal to the subconscious, resulted in an eroticism far more potent than that induced by any amount of full-frontal writhing. Passion gained intensity in proportion to its postponement and Screen Lovers' emotions were constantly being heightened by enforced separations, by selfless renunciation and by sickness and death. If there was physical consummation of the relationship, it was usually restricted to a clinch and a kiss, and the rest, of necessity, was left to the audience's imagination.

In the Seventies, when the explicit sex scene became a requisite feature of any onscreen relationship, the distinction between love and sex might have seemed to disappear. In fact the boundary was only reinforced. At its best, the sex scene added a new dimension to the interaction between Screen Lovers, but more often it was simply a mechanical, emotion-free interlude inserted into the narrative in order to conform to box-office trends. Barely relevant to the plots that surrounded it, sex became divorced and distinct not only from love, but also from the rest of life.

In the earlier, less 'liberated' days of the cinema, the fact that explicit sex was forbidden meant that, in actuality, the possibility of it was always there, hovering just out of frame in the spectator's head. It is one of the age-old paradoxes of eroticism: less means more. The sight of Jack Nicholson and Jessica Lange writhing around on the kitchen table in the explicit 1981 remake of *The Postman Always Rings Twice* turns out to be far less suggestive of all-consuming lust than the deliberately repressed emotions (all pursed lips and conspiratorial glances) of Lana Turner and John Garfield, their 1946 counterparts.

Time plays strange tricks on Screen Lovers. Theda Bara with her kohl-rimmed eyes and theatrical vamping might seem to us now a hopelessly antiquated vision. The films of Janet Gaynor and Charles Farrell might appear impossibly naive, and those of Jeanette MacDonald and Nelson Eddy ridiculously camp. Films which condemned fallen women to a lifetime of degradation and selfless renunciation, whereas the men in their lives were permitted to go unchecked from one conquest to the next, might raise hackles when viewed in the light of today's post-feminist sensibilities. But it requires only a small imaginative leap for us to enjoy such movies in the spirit in which they were originally intended. And the classics, constructed as they are around some basic emotional truth, continue to touch us where it counts.

Screen Lovers might look different nowadays. Their *modus operandi* and the words that they whisper (or sometimes yell) to each other have varied through the years. But they are still going strong up there on the screen and their influence, past and present, continues to pervade our lives. The cinema has its leading men and ladies, but their individual careers would be unthinkable without the reaction and attraction that links them together. Their mutual rapport, which reaches out to embrace us, the audience, is the strongest emotional bond that cinema has to offer. We are privileged voyeurs indeed.

Clark Gable and Joan Crawford in Possessed (1931)
One of the eight movies they made together. This is the film in which, despite beating up Joan Crawford and calling her a 'little tramp', Gable enhanced his popularity with female moviegoers.
Photographer: George Hurrell

THE
SEVEN AGES
THE SILENTS

The earliest Screen Lovers were imported from live theatre and brought with them the conventions of Victorian melodrama. Characters were stereotypes of Good and Bad. True Love was a reward for virtue and sex the province of wicked men and women, who used it to lure good characters from the straight and narrow. A vital movie-making rule was established: audiences preferred their moral messages to be wrapped in hefty helpings of titillation. Virtue might be ultimately triumphant, but it was Vice, depicted in all its lurid detail, which caught the public imagination.

Seductiveness was *not* one of the all-American virtues. Hollywood created the Exotic Outsider to fit the role of Bad Girl, or Vamp. Theodosia Goodman, a tailor's daughter from Cincinnati, was transformed into Theda Bara, and Rheatha Watson from Richmond, Virginia, became Barbara La Marr. As far as Hollywood was concerned, foreign parts, and particularly Paris, were synonymous with sexual licence: film-makers had only to insert a stock shot of the Eiffel Tower into their studio-bound action for the audience to realize that whatever followed would be hot stuff.

By the end of World War One, audiences had tired of straightforward dramas of Good and Bad and demanded something more sophisticated. Cecil B. De Mille gave them social comedies such as *Don't Change Your Husband* (1919) and *Why Change Your Wife?* (1920) and made a star out of Gloria Swanson. De Mille's contemporary tales of adultery were cut with flashbacks to the fleshpots of ancient Babylon and Rome, allowing him to drum home a few homilies while dabbling in orgy sequences.

European film-makers were more daring than their Hollywood counterparts. German films such as Karl Grune's *Die Strasse/The Street* (1923) were crammed with realistic depictions of lowlife and immorality. The nearest equivalent that Hollywood could offer in reply was the work of Erich Von Stroheim, whose *Foolish Wives* (1922) and *The Merry Widow* (1925) revelled in lechery and perversion, though their decadence was offset by keen psychological insight.

Gloria Swanson in Why Change Your Wife? (1920)
The swankiest of the silent stars in one of Cecil B. De Mille's popular social comedies.

Vilma Banky and Rudolph Valentino in The Son of the Sheik (1926)
The screen's first major male sex symbol in his last film.

Sexual passion remained the province of the Exotic Outsider. Hollywood's first male sexual icon was Rudolph Valentino, who was a world away from the polite, all-American leading man typified by Harold Lockwood or Conrad Nagel. As Arab, Argentinian and Frenchman, Valentino wooed his women in grand style, kissing hands with a suggestive glance and intimating, in films like *The Four Horsemen of the Apocalypse* (1921) and *The Sheik* (1921), that whatever he wanted he would take, by force if necessary. On the distaff side, Swedish-born Greta Garbo specialized in the portrayal of fallen women and temptresses in films such as *Flesh and the Devil* (1927) and *A Woman of Affairs* (1928).

American girls had to be content with 'It'. This was supposed to be that indefinable something possessed by the new breed of liberated young women, the flappers and career girls of the Roaring Twenties. Clara Bow starred in *It* (1927) and became the 'It' girl, an epithet coined by Elinor Glyn, self-styled romantic expert and author of *Three Weeks* (a Ruritanian romance which had been filmed in 1924, inspiring a flood of imitations).

▲ **Norma Shearer and Ramon Novarro in The Student Prince/The Student Prince in Old Heidelburg (1927)**
The prince and the commoner say it with flowers. Ernst Lubitsch's charming silent version of Sigmund Romberg's operetta.

▶ **Theda Bara in Cleopatra (1917)**
The charm of the Exotic Outsider. Cinema's first *femme fatale* plays history's favourite temptress.

THE SEVEN AGES
THE THIRTIES

The first talkies added an important new weapon to the Screen Lover's arsenal of seduction: the voice. It also weeded out those whose vocals failed to match up to their image. Squeaky-voiced heroes were *out,* as were romantic heroines with the vowel sounds of a Brooklyn shopgirl. Sound also taxed the ingenuity of scriptwriters: what might have seemed the ultimate in smouldering desire when related via intertitles was often absurd when spoken out loud.

Screen Lovers provided escapism during the Depression. They also cropped up in social dramas and gangster films, and though the line between Good Girl and Bad was less clearly defined, it still existed. Somewhere in the middle was the independent career girl who found work as secretary, shop assistant or chorus girl. As always, illicit passion was a more popular theme than wedded bliss; adultery and pre-marital sex might never have been condoned, but they sure as hell provided a lot of plots. In the comedy, the visual slapstick of the silents was now supplemented by verbal wisecracking, perfected in the best of the screwball funnies, where one character's life was turned upside down by the intrusion of madcap romance.

German-born Marlene Dietrich joined Garbo in the ranks of Hollywood's exotic imports to play *femmes fatales* and fallen women. But sex took centre stage in the film of some American stars too: home-grown hussies like Jean Harlow (who dispensed with such niceties as underwear) and Mae West, whose brazen enjoyment of the men in her life (and the life in her men) outraged organizations such as the Catholic Legion of Decency.

The Motion Picture Producers and Distributors of America (the MPPDA) ratified the Production Code in an attempt to stem what it saw as a rising tide of licentiousness. The Code decreed that the sanctity of marriage and the home should be upheld, that 'scenes of passion should not be introduced when not instrumental to the plot', that 'excessive and lustful kissing' should be avoided and that 'seduction or rape should never be more than suggested'. Husbands and wives could legitimately be seen together in their bedrooms, provided they slept in twin beds. Crime or adultery could not go unpunished: if the heroine was a fallen woman, then she had either to die or repent and reform. Films were vetted from first treatment to final print, and Hollywood pandered to these stipulations until the mid Sixties.

In wicked Europe, however, there were no such petty restrictions. Whores, pimps and other denizens of lowlife were depicted with a candour undreamt of in the United States. In the French gangster movie *Pépé le Moko* (1937), Mireille Balin played the kept woman of an older man; Hedy Lamarr's role in *Algiers*, the 1938 Hollywood remake, was amended to that of fiancée.

Gary Cooper and Merle Oberon in The Cowboy and the Lady (1938)
The *Grande Dame* and the Rodeo Star: love means never having to worry about whether your lifestyles are compatible. *Photographer: Bob Coburn*

24

**Benita Hulme, Merle Oberon, Douglas Fairbanks, Joan Gardner and (sitting)
Elsa Lanchester in The Private Life of Don Juan (1934)**
The legendary lover flanked by females who conveniently ignore the fact that the actor is getting
rather long in the tooth; it was Fairbanks's last film.

Marlene Dietrich in Shanghai Express (1932)
The Exotic Outsider kitted out with the trappings of seduction: a feather boa, gloves and a cigarette.

▲ Bette Davis and Paul Henreid in Now, Voyager (1942)

The spinster and the married man reach a starry-eyed romantic compromise in one of the classic women's pictures.

▼ Mary Astor and Herbert Marshall in Young Ideas (1943)

The twin room syndrome. The Hollywood Production Code stipulated separate beds for married couples.

THE
SEVEN AGES
THE FIFTIES

After an evident burst of feminine self-sufficiency during the war years, there was a tacit drive to entice women back into the home, leaving the workplace free for the returning heroes. The spunky career girl was a thing of the past. Movies depicted females either as wives and mothers or as curvaceous cuties: Marilyn Monroe, Jayne Mansfield and Mamie Van Doren promulgated the image of woman as a sexpot with very little brain. Britain jumped onto the bandwagon with Diana Dors, but the European equivalent, exemplified by Sophia Loren, Brigitte Bardot and Gina Lollobrigida, was somehow earthier and less homogenized. Although some of these actresses were later to prove themselves capable of more than mere posing and pouting, in the Fifties there was a marked lack of the sassy sexual brass once displayed by the likes of Mae West and Jean Harlow.

The influence of the major Hollywood studios was on the wane, due partly to far-reaching changes within the film distribution system. Moreover, film-makers were now competing against television; they explored exotic locations and newly developed technology (such as 3-D and CinemaScope) in an effort to lure audiences away from the upstart medium. Screen Lovers were sometimes swamped by the resultant gimmickry, but they flourished in certain genres. The edgy relationship between the hero and an erotic, ice-cool blonde became a regular fixture of Alfred Hitchcock's thrillers. Douglas Sirk, whose *Magnificent Obsession* (1954) and *Imitation of Life* (1959) were glossy remakes of John M. Stahl's Thirties melodramas, elevated soap-opera into high-camp art. Fritz Lang's *Rancho Notorious* (1952), Nicholas Ray's *Johnny Guitar* (1954) and Samuel Fuller's *Forty Guns* (1957), featured women (Marlene Dietrich, Joan Crawford and Barbara Stanwyck respectively) in unusually prominent roles and gave a new romantic impetus to the western.

Otto Preminger successfully challenged the authority of the Production Code with *The Moon Is Blue* (1953), the screenplay of which featured such taboo words as 'pregnant' and 'virgin'. The steamy sexual frustration of Tennessee Williams's plays was toned down for the screen, but the

Marilyn Monroe and Tony Curtis in Some Like It Hot (1959)
A fine example of the fifties' predeliction for curvaceous cuties. In Billy Wilder's cross-dressing comedy, Monroe is so addle-brained that she doesn't recognise her lover when he's wearing a frock.

films of *Cat on a Hot Tin Roof* (1958) and *Suddenly Last Summer* (1959) could still hint at homosexual proclivities. Black actors, who had previously been confined to playing servants or musicians, could now, very occasionally, land roles as Screen Lovers in films such as Preminger's all-black *Carmen Jones* (1954). Robert Rossen's *Island in the Sun* (1957) was a rare instance of interracial romance, something that to this day remains virtually non-existent in American films.

For the first time, the teenager was identified as a box-office force to be reckoned with. In America's post-war boom, young people found themselves with real spending power and a culture of their own. The movie theatre or drive-in cinema was a popular sanctuary away from the sphere of parental influence. The great screen teams of the Thirties and Forties gave way to new idols: loners and rebels such as James Dean and Marlon Brando. Teenagers weren't interested in grand passion; Screen Lovers were, at best, peripheral in the new wave of anti-authoritarian, rock 'n' roll, or sci-fi pictures which catered for this new market.

▲Mary Murphy (3rd left) and Marlon Brando in The Wild One (1954)
Question: 'What're you rebelling against?' Reply: 'What've you got?' The rebel loner takes centre
stage and love interest falls by the wayside.

►Troy Donahue and Sandra Dee in A Summer Place (1959)
Teen-dream romance with a hint of soap.

**Gloria Swanson and William Holden in Sunset
Boulevard (1950)**
The faded silent movie-star who adopts a hard-bitten hack as
her toy boy.

**Harry Belafonte and Joan Fontaine in Island in the Sun
(1957)**
A rare occurrence in Hollywood movies. Romance between a
black and a white person.

▶**Elizabeth Taylor in Cat on a Hot Tin Roof (1958)**
A solitary Lover in the film of Tennessee Williams's play.

THE
SEVEN AGES
THE SIXTIES

Hollywood was in trouble. The big studios were struggling for survival. Domestic comedies starring the likes of Doris Day appeared hopelessly outmoded compared to foreign product from the French New Wave and the new British 'permissive' cinema, in which soft-focus escapism gave way to gritty realism, and sexual relationships were depicted with an unprecedented candour. British films such as *Victim* (1961) and *A Taste of Honey* (1961) attempted to treat homosexuals sympathetically, whereas heterosexual partners were there to be bedded and discarded in *Darling* (1965), *Alfie* (1966) and – in lighter vein – the James Bond films. The bleak visions of Italy's Michelangelo Antonioni and the gloomy Swede Ingmar Bergman explored the gulfs between Screen Lovers; Bergman's *The Silence* (1963) depicted lesbianism, incest and masturbation (the last solace of the frustrated Screen Lover).

Skinflicks, formerly stag-party fodder, began to nose their way into polite society. Few regular moviegoers might have seen the Swedish movie *I Am Curious – Yellow* (1963), but most had at least heard of or read about it. Andy Warhol's underground movies exploited the varied and numerous sexual proclivities of his protégés and co-workers, presenting full-frontal nudity (both male and female) and prostitution as facts of life.

Love interest was no longer restricted to a single co-star: Elvis Presley had *Girls! Girls! Girls!* (1962), and a bevy of bikini-clad lovelies was essential to any self-respecting spy thriller. Explicit sex scenes began to infiltrate mainstream Hollywood, and in 1966 the Production Code was revised to accommodate films such as *The Graduate* (1967), in which a married woman seduces a younger man, *Goodbye Columbus* (1969) which brought contraception in on the act, and *Midnight Cowboy* (1969), which featured male prostitution.

Steve McQueen and Natalie Wood in Love With the Proper Stranger (1963)
Serious kissing manoeuvres.

▶ **Beryl Reid and Susannah York in The Killing of Sister George (1968)**
A lesbian love affair.

▼ **Shirley Anne Field and Albert Finney in Saturday Night and Sunday Morning (1960)**
The screen rebel, British-style. The Angry Young Man and his not-so-angry girl.

**Michael Caine with Vivien Merchant, Jane Asher, Julia Foster and Shelley Winters
in Alfie (1966)**
One is not enough: the bachelor boy and his harem.

▲Monica Vitti and Alain Delon in L'Eclisse/Eclipse (1962)
Alienation Italian-style. One of Michelangelo Antonioni's films which expresses the futility of love and life, lacking in plot.

▼Jean-Paul Belmondo and Anna Karina in Pierrot le Fou (1965)
Screen Lovers all at sea on the crest of the sixties' French New Wave.

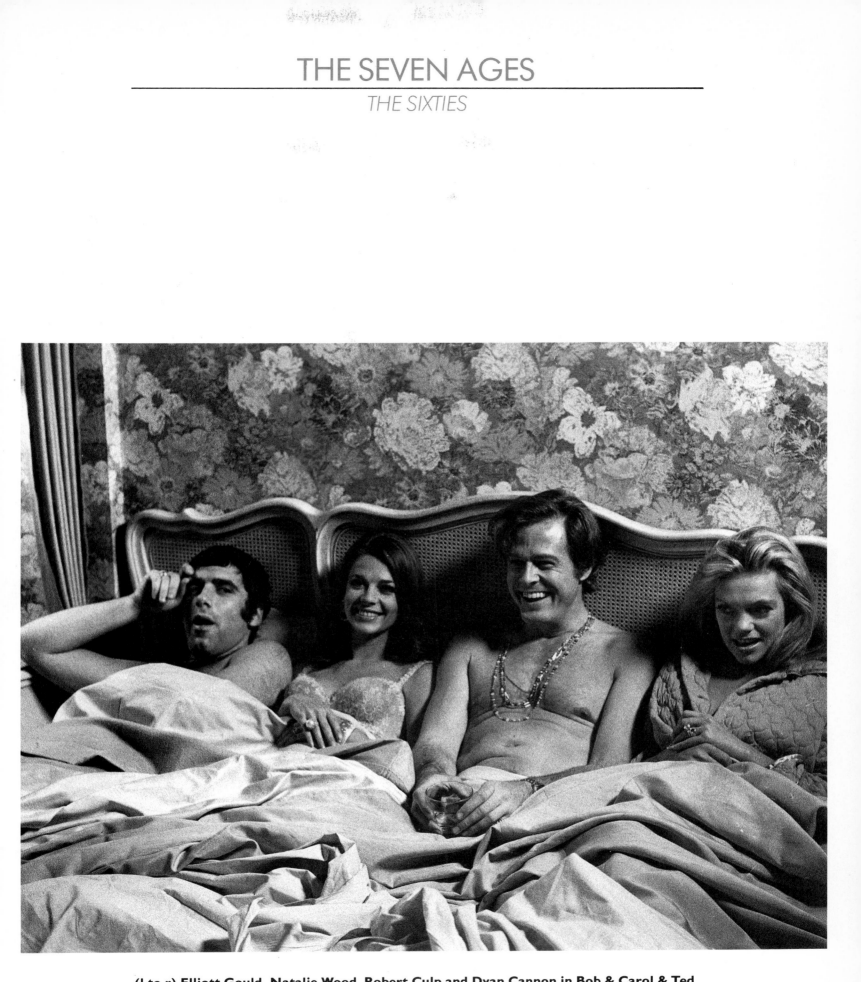

(l to r) Elliott Gould, Natalie Wood, Robert Culp and Dyan Cannon in Bob & Carol & Ted & Alice (1969)
Four's company: modern love, partner-swapping and cheap laundry bills.

HUMPHREY BOGART
Across the Pacific
MARY ASTOR · SYDNEY GREENSTREET
Directed by JOHN HUSTON
SCREEN PLAY BY RICHARD MACAULAY FROM THE SATURDAY EVENING POST SERIAL BY ROBERT CARSON
A WARNER BROS.- FIRST NATIONAL PICTURE
Presented by WARNER BROS.

THE
SEVEN AGES
THE SEVENTIES

The Seventies were the heyday of the 'Buddy Movie'; romantic interest became redundant in these hymns to male camaraderie. Occasional attempts to revive romance were isolated amidst a welter of special effects and slam-bang action. Pictures with strong female leads were rare; the sexual revolution of the Sixties had somehow resulted in the devaluation of the female partner, rather than her liberation. As far as film-makers were concerned, there was little distinction between love and sex, and there were few movies aimed at adults which did not include at least one scene of naked bodies and sweaty limbs intertwined.

The gap between smut and mainstream was closing up fast. Sex became chic: moviegoers who in an earlier decade would never have been seen dead near a porno theatre flocked to see *Deep Throat* (1972), the hardcore fellatio film that everyone was talking about. *Emmanuelle* (1974) gave sex a high-gloss, soft-focus finish that made it suitable (if not serious) entertainment for respectable couples.

A boom in independent movie theatres catered to a revived interest in classic Hollywood films and their stars. Bogart and Bacall, Tracy and Hepburn, Monroe, Dean, all proved to have timeless box-office appeal, their popularity perhaps indicating that contemporary cinema was failing to come up with the goods. The film industry succumbed to a fit of nostalgia in an effort to give the punters what they wanted: *American Graffiti* (1973), *The Sting* (1973) and *The Great Gatsby* (1974) all harked back to what now seemed like golden eras. The renewed popularity of the old guard was never more obvious than in *Play It Again, Sam* (1972), where the shadow of Humphrey Bogart pops up at regular intervals to advise Woody Allen on how best to use old-fashioned chat-up lines to woo Diane Keaton.

Woody Allen and Diane Keaton in Play It Again, Sam (1972)
Taking tips from Humphrey Bogart, the shades of old movies loom large.

▲Robert Redford and Mia Farrow in The Great Gatsby (1974)
Screen Lovers caught up in the mid-Seventies' nostalgia boom: an uninspiring adaptation of F. Scott Fitzgerald's novel.

▲▲Margot Kidder and Christopher Reeve in Superman (1978)
Here, the ever-popular comic-strip Screen Lovers reach new heights with special effects.

Sam Neill and Judy Davis in My Brilliant Career (1979)
Australian Screen Lovers. The story of a young woman's emancipation, this film became an
unexpected art-house hit.

THE
SEVEN AGES
THE EIGHTIES

By the start of the Eighties, the cinema was catering for a predominantly young audience. The coming-of-age teenpic proliferated, as did the *Friday the 13th* cycle of horror films, curious cautionary tales in which young people who dared to have sex were promptly butchered by a psychopathic murderer. But there were signs that films about adult relationships were making a comeback, and, in movies such as *Lianna* (1983), *My Beautiful Laundrette* (1985), *Desert Hearts* (1985) and *Maurice* (1987), that homosexuality was no longer being treated as an aberration. Even the teenpic eventually matured under the auspices of John Hughes, who in *The Breakfast Club* (1985) attempted to treat his young characters as real people instead of sex-mad slobs.

It is still too early to gauge the full effect of AIDS on the film industry, but there are indications that casual sex will no longer be considered a harmless pursuit. Whereas we are unlikely to regress as far as having twin beds for married couples, there is a possibility that the subject of sex might be approached in a more responsible and realistic manner: a scene in *Dragnet* (1987), for example, shows Tom Hanks saying no to intercourse because he's run out of condoms, while in *Broadcast News* (1987), Holly Hunter slips a packet of prophylactics into her handbag before a date with William Hurt.

The New Morality was beginning to make itself felt in other ways. Films such as *Fatal Attraction* (1987) were modern variations on the moral that those who dabble in infidelity will be punished for their sins. In the so-called 'yuppie nightmare' movies, of which *After Hours* (1985), *Blue Velvet* (1986) and *Something Wild* (1986) were the most noteworthy examples, women were once more being cast as predatory *femmes fatales*, luring straitlaced men into dangerous situations in a synthesis of screwball comedy and *film noir*.

The British film industry, meanwhile, was showing reluctance to deal with relationships in a contemporary setting. Movies such as *Dance with a Stranger* (1985), *Sid and Nancy* (1986), *Prick Up Your Ears* (1987) and *White Mischief* (1988) were all real-life stories set in the (albeit quite recent) past, and each ended in death for one or both of the Screen Lovers. When relationships *were* set in the present, they tended to be indigestible slabs of sexual and social agitprop, like *Sammy and Rosie Get Laid* (1987).

Michael Douglas and Glenn Close in Fatal Attraction (1987)
The dangers of straying from the straight and narrow: this woman refuses to let go when her married lover returns to his wife and child. One of the most talked-about films of the Eighties.

Nevertheless, it was apparent from the mid Eighties onwards that Screen Lovers were back in force after the doldrums of the past decade, although few films had the nerve to present themselves as out-and-out romance. Those that did, such as *Falling in Love* (1984), fell flat, despite the presence of bankable stars. Love stories now came heavily disguised: *Stakeout* (1987), *The Big Easy* (1987), and *Someone To Watch Over Me* (1987) masqueraded as thrillers, although a romantic relationship is central to each. *Witness* (1985) was another romantic thriller, *Out of Africa* (1985) a biographical romance, *A Room with a View* (1985) a literary romance, *Betty Blue* (1986) a study of *amour fou*, and *Crocodile Dundee* (1986) a romantic comedy. Screen Lovers even infiltrated the special-effects sci-fi movie: the protagonists of both *Back to the Future* (1985) and *Peggy Sue Got Married* (1986) travelled back in time to sort out emotional tangles. War films such as *Platoon* (1986) and *Full Metal Jacket* (1987) might have been totally lacking in Screen Lovers, but there is evidence to suggest that the rest of cinema still has plenty of room for the romantic relationship.

Richard Gere and Debra Winger in An Officer and a Gentleman (1981)
Although Gere's popularity later waned rapidly after he appeared in a string of flops, in this film he demonstrated the sex appeal of military uniforms and big motorbikes.

Back row (l to r): JoBeth Williams, Tom Berenger, Glenn Close, Kevin Kline, Mary Kay Place and front row: William Hurt, Meg Tilly, Jeff Goldblum in The Big Chill (1983)
Partner-swapping revisited. Close encourages her husband (Kline) to sleep with her best friend.

Sean Young and Kevin Kostner in No Way Out (1987)

The Hollywood thriller, Eighties-style: a remake of *The Big Clock* (1948) with added sex scenes. *Photographer: S. Karin Epstein*

Charles Dance and Greta Scacchi in White Mischief (1988)

British colonials leading a dissolute life in Forties-Kenya: an adaptation of James Fox's book about real-life adultery and murder in East Africa.

Cher and Nicolas Cage in Moonstruck (1987)
A return to the heartwarming romantic comedy. Cher, who won an Oscar for her performance, falls
in love with her absent fiancé's brother (Cage) and lives happily ever after in Little Italy.

THE
BIG COMBO
GREAT SCREEN TEAMS

The Big Combos: their names go together like salt and pepper, snap and crackle, love and marriage. Many of the great movie partnerships, like those of Tracy and Hepburn or Bogart and Bacall, were conducted offscreen as well as on, and are the subject of Private Lives (page 87). But others were played out purely for the benefit of the public. Audiences liked what they saw and wanted more of the same, and the studios could be relied upon to cash in on the money-raking magic of a winning team. 'That incomparable pair are back!' trumpeted the blurb for Myrna Loy and William Powell's latest outing. Or 'Reunion – In Love – By Request' as the publicity machine heralded another of Clark Gable and Joan Crawford's outings together.

The first screen teams surfaced in the comic shorts and serials churned out during the silent era. But the first major romantic combo was that of Ronald Colman and the Hungarian actress Vilma Banky, who were brought together by producer Samuel Goldwyn to star in the World War One drama *The Dark Angel* (1925). Banky's blonde loveliness was the perfect complement to Colman's dashing good looks, and the duo made four other movies together before their popularity began to wane, partly as a result of Banky's well-publicized marriage to a third party, actor Rod La Rocque.

The heady embraces of Colman and Banky seemed almost the model of chastity when compared to the white-hot passions displayed by Greta Garbo and John Gilbert, who were lovers offscreen as well as on. Less torrid in their approach, but no less popular, were Janet Gaynor and Charles Farrell. Their first three films, all directed by Frank Borzage, summed up the duo's appeal: pure love triumphing over the slings and arrows of dreary existence and melodramatic plotlines.

In *Seventh Heaven* (1927), Farrell played a Parisian sewage worker who becomes enamoured of Gaynor's tattered gamine before being blinded in World War One, to be sustained by his loved one's waiflike devotion. The pair were angels with dirty faces and, if Gaynor's reputation was less than spotless in films such as *Street Angel* (1928), it was only because she had

Humphrey Bogart and Lauren Bacall in Dark Passage (1947)
Private lives leaking out onto the big screen, a Big Combo behind the scenes as well as on celluloid.

Ronald Colman and Vilma Banky in Two Lovers (1928)
One of the first great screen teams, 'The Hungarian Rhapsody'
and her British Beau.

compromised her purity to provide medicine for her poor sick mother. The Borzage films were by far the best of the tearjerking twosome's twelve appearances together. Though excessively sentimental by today's standards, these films have a simple sincerity that is far more effective than the cynical manipulation found in more recent sob-fests such as *Kramer vs. Kramer* (1979) and *Terms of Endearment* (1983).

The Thirties and Forties were the heyday of the Great Screen Team. Audiences sought romance and glamour as a means of escaping from the depressing political and economic reality and they found it in spades. Clark Gable assumed the mantle of rugged screen manliness and dabbled in successful teamwork with Joan Crawford, Jean Harlow, Myrna Loy and Lana Turner, although it was his one-off role as the wisecracking reporter opposite Claudette Colbert in *It Happened One Night* (1934) that copped him his only Academy Award, and it was as Rhett Butler to Vivien Leigh's Scarlett O'Hara (another one-off) in *Gone With the Wind* (1939) that his immortality was assured. Female filmgoers were fed up with the polite heroes of the early talkie 'teacup dramas'. Gable was rough and tough; he could behave in the most cavalier fashion towards his leading ladies, even slap their faces, and get away with it. Offscreen, his marriage to the enormously popular Carole Lombard cemented his status as a Screen Lover of the first order.

Fred Astaire's austere elegance was offset by the sex appeal of the archetypal snappy broad, Ginger Rogers, who always gave the impression of having made it up through the chorusline to be lady for a day, swept away into a happy-ever-after world of temporary misunder-standing and misalliance. The plots of films such as *Top Hat* (1935) and *Swing Time* (1936) were the flimsiest of excuses on which to hang a series of dance set-pieces that were almost erotic in their precision: two individuals welded together in perfectly synchronized step. Astaire had other, more skilful partners, but these were as so many casual flirtations; with Rogers, it was the Real Thing.

Jeanette MacDonald dallied with Maurice Chevalier in several movies, as well as with Clark Gable, but her shrill soprano will be forever bonded to the baritone of Nelson Eddy. From a cynical viewpoint, their sugary-sweet operettas might appear to be no more than a watering-down of grand opera's heavy-duty passions into a format suitable for mass consumption. But 'America's Sweet-hearts', as they were known, warbled their way into film history as the most successful screen singing-team ever. Their films, loaded with frills, trills and blossom, are fine examples of tearjerking high camp.

On a less frothy front, director W. S. Van Dyke rescued Myrna Loy from a lifetime of being cast as Fu Manchu's daughter and pitted her against William Powell in *The Thin*

Continued on page 61

Janet Gaynor and Charles Farrell in Tess of the Storm Country (1932)
America's favourite lovebirds. Even when their films were set in the gutter, they projected sweetness, light, and wholesome sentiment. *Photographer: Hal Phyfe*

▲ Clark Gable and Jean Harlow in Red Dust (1932)
The Screen Lover (male) has a longer career than the Screen Lover (female). Gable was to repeat this role 21 years later in *Mogambo*, with Ava Gardner filling in for Harlow.

▶ Margaret Sullavan and James Stewart in The Shop Around the Corner (1940)
Ernst Lubitsch's charming tale of romantic penpals in Budapest. In real life, Stewart had a big crush on Sullavan.

George Brent and Bette Davis in Dark Victory (1939)
The brain surgeon and the terminally ill socialite: Brent was an object lesson in the subjugation of an
actor's ego to the scene-stealing, top-billed Davis. *Photographer: Shuyler Crail*

Man (1934) and its sequels. This blend of detective drama and screwball comedy, though having little in common with Dashiell Hammett's original story, was a spectacular commercial success. Powell and Loy, as Nick and Nora Charles, became everyone's idea of a well-heeled married couple, knocking back quantities of liquor in a flurry of well-aimed wisecracks and solving a murder or two on the side. Powell did most of the legwork, it's true, but at least Loy kept up the pretence of being an equal partner in a liberated marriage. It was a far better deal than was available to most film wives, who tended to be frumpy individuals whose existence was a barrier to true love rather than a constituent of it.

Starting on *42nd Street* (1933), Ruby Keeler hoofed her way into the public's heart via those masterpieces of saucy symbolism, the Busby Berkeley musicals. Ever the fresh-faced innocent unaffected by the showbiz bawdiness surrounding her, she was repeatedly serenaded by the eager Dick Powell, who managed to radiate health and good clean lust in equal amounts.

Screen Lovers have a thankless task in the costumed action picture, lumbered as they are with essentially one-dimensional roles and unappreciated by an audience which is waiting impatiently for the next bout of swashbuckling, spear-chucking or Cherokee-bashing. But Olivia De Havil-

land exuded a sweet-faced sincerity which made her ideally suited to play Errol Flynn's love interest in historical romances such as *Captain Blood* (1935) and *The Adventures of Robin Hood* (1938). Flynn, married in real life to actress Lili Damita, developed a big crush on his co-star during the making of *The Charge of the Light Brigade* (1936) but, lacking the sensitive touch, could only express his feelings via stunts such as hiding a dead snake in her dressing room. The lady, not surprisingly, remained aloof.

Margaret Sullavan and James Stewart appeared in four films together. The last of these, *The Mortal Storm* (1940), was directed by Frank Borzage, whose *Seventh Heaven* (1927) had rocketed the Gaynor and Farrell combo to fame. Indeed, the teaming of Sullavan and Stewart was almost an update of the earlier duo, aimed at an audience which was no longer prepared to put up with schlock, but which nonetheless liked a good, sentimental wallow. Stewart, like Farrell, towered over his tiny co-star and the two of them portrayed nice, ordinary people whose lives are torn by the convolutions of Fate. Sullavan's husky-voiced vulnerability and Stewart's gee-whizz gawkiness were perfectly matched, and audiences were duly touched by their credible displays of shy affection.

Tyrone Power and Loretta Young were a brace of filmstar faces with no ragged edges, offering personality-

◄Olivia De Havilland and Errol Flynn in The Adventures of Robin Hood (1938)
A romantic interlude amongst the swashbuckling scenes. Even action heroes need a bit of love interest
on the side. *Photographer: Mac Julian*

Joan Blondell and James Cagney in He Was Her Man (1934)
Despite co-starring in several films, these two never made it into the ranks of the great screen teams. He made a name for himself in lone-wolf roles, while she was forever being cast as the brassy, sassy chorus-girl type.

Ginger Rogers and Fred Astaire in Swing Time (1936)
Hollywood's top dancers caught with their feet on the ground for a change.

free romance in such airy confections as *Love Is News* (1937) and *Café Metropole* (1937). Through the late Thirties and early Forties, Judy Garland and Mickey Rooney exuded hyperactive exuberance as youthful Screen Lovers suitable for all the family, bubbling their way through various Andy Hardy yarns and putting-on-a-show numbers as though they had been force-fed on dairy products. Donald O'Connor and Peggy Ryan bounced irrepressibly in their wake, followed by John Payne and Betty Grable, Danny Kaye and Virginia Mayo, all of them seemingly limitless reservoirs of musical energy.

Greer Garson and Walter Pidgeon represented noble forbearance, particularly in *Mrs Miniver* (1942), Hollywood's hymn to the British war effort. Alan Ladd and Veronica Lake were a small but perfectly formed blond combo in thrillers such as *This Gun for Hire* (1942) and *The*

Glass Key (1942). Jon Hall and Maria Montez catered to the American taste for camp exotica with films such as *White Savage* (1943) and *Cobra Woman* (1944). Across the Atlantic, Anna Neagle and Michael Wilding appeared in a string of popular romances with titles like *Piccadilly Incident* (1946) and *Maytime in Mayfair* suggesting an obsession with the expensive end of the Monopoly board.

Then there were the comedy couples, homely types that reassured the public that romance need not be restricted to screen gods and goddesses: Marie Dressler and Wallace Beery, Charlie Ruggles and Mary Boland, Slim Summerville and ZaSu Pitts. Groucho Marx baited the ever-

Loretta Young and Tyrone Power in Cafe Metropole (1937)
A smooth and toothsome twosome.

Continued on page 69

Nelson Eddy and Jeanette MacDonald in The Girl of the Golden West (1938)
America's singing sweethearts in full romantic swing in a never-never land full of bittersweet duets
and picturesque backdrops.

Gracie Allen and George Burns in a publicity portrait (c. 1935)
Just a couple of kooks: a husband and wife team which clowned about on stage, screen and airwaves.

Gary Cooper and Jean Arthur in Mr Deeds Goes to Town (1936)
Frank Capra's sharp social comedy with an appealing soft centre. Arthur's hardboiled reporter was
the perfect foil for Cooper's *faux-naif* millionaire. These two also starred together in *The Plainsman*
(1936), in which he was Wild Bill Hickok to her Calamity Jane.

William Powell and Myrna Loy in Another Thin Man (1939)
Nick and Nora Charles, perfect married partners, with Asta
the wire-haired fox terrier as surrogate child.

Ruby Keeler and Dick Powell in Gold Diggers of 1933 (1933)
Fresh-faced innocence amongst Busby Berkeley's saucy showgirl routines.

Johnny Weissmuller and Maureen O'Sullivan in *Tarzan and His Mate* (1934)
Jungle lovers in matching loincloths, Weissmuller and O'Sullivan are the best-remembered of the
many celluloid incarnations of Tarzan and Jane.

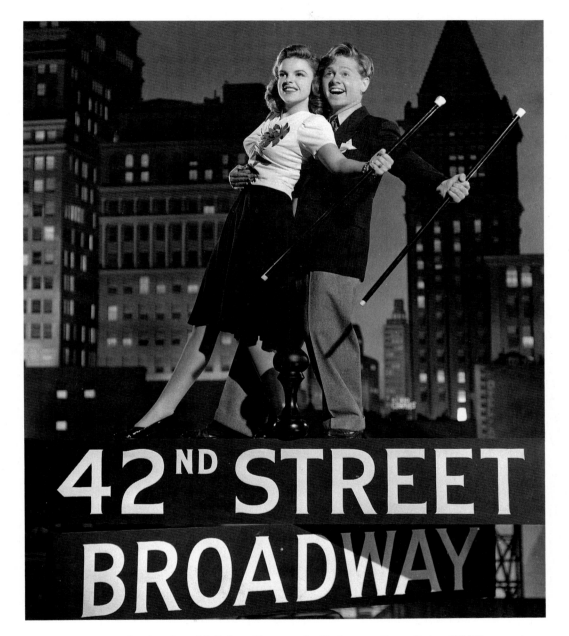

Judy Garland and Mickey Rooney in Babes on Broadway (1941)

patient Margaret Dumont with outrageous double entendres and finely-honed insults. Marjorie Main and Percy Kilbride scored such a hit in the supporting cast of *The Egg and I* (1947) that their hillbilly characters, Ma and Pa Kettle, were given their very own film series.

Penny Singleton and Arthur Lake brought Chic Young's comic strip to life in the long-running *Blondie* series (28 daffy domestic comedies between 1938 and 1950) and Laraine Day brought romance to Blair General Hospital as Lew Ayres's fiancée in the *Dr Kildare* films (1938–47). Buster Crabbe and Jean Rogers took Screen Lovers into outer space in the *Flash Gordon* serial (1938–40), and a loincloth-clad Johnny Weissmuller yodelled his way into

Maureen O'Sullivan's heart in *Tarzan the Ape Man* (1932) and a clutch of follow-ups. 'He knew only the law of the jungle – to seize what he wanted!' exclaimed the publicist's blurb, making the monkey man sound like the most rapacious Screen Lover since Valentino.

With the gradual collapse of the studio system in the Fifties and Sixties, Hollywood stars were no longer at the mercy of rigid contracts. They began to exercise more control over their own careers and became reluctant to be slotted into typecast pairings. The Big Combo virtually disappeared from the cinema screen. Television serials and soaps were the new breeding grounds for long-running romantic teams, some of them featuring erstwhile film

Continued on page 82

▲Alan Ladd and Veronica Lake in The Blue Dahlia (1946)
The small but perfectly-formed blond combo in a murder mystery scripted by Raymond Chandler.

▶Cary Grant and Irene Dunne in My Favorite Wife (1940)
Sophisticated, witty Screen Lovers in a fine marital mix-up. *Photographer: Fred Hendrickson*

Percy Kilbride and Marjorie Main (centre) in Ma and Pa Kettle at the Fair (1952)
The hillbilly twosome in one of a series of films which pre-dated *The Beverly Hillbillies*, a television series of their adventures.

Douglas Dumbrille, Margaret Dumont and Groucho Marx in The Big Store (1941)
The long-suffering Dumont gets it in the neck from Groucho yet again.

Robert Young, Laraine Day, Lew Ayres and Lionel Barrymore in Dr Kildare's Crisis (1940)
One of Paramount's long-running series set in Blair General Hospital. Day, as Nurse Mary Lamont,
played Dr Kildare's love interest.

Arthur Lake, Penny Singleton and Larry Simms in Blondie Takes a Vacation (1939)
One of a series of films inspired by Chic Young's popular comic-strip characters: Dagwood Bumstead,
his wife Blondie and their child Baby Dumpling, plus Daisy the Dog. *Photographer: 'Whitey' Shafer*

▲ **Danny Kaye and Virginia Mayo in A Song Is Born (1948)**
Howard Hawks's musical remake of his own film *Ball of Fire* (1941)

▼ **Donald O'Connor and Peggy Ryan in Patrick the Great (1944)**
The all-singing, all-dancing teen-team in an entertainment for all the family.

Anna Neagle and Michael Wilding in Spring in Park Lane (1948)
Snob appeal for the masses.

▲**Greer Garson and Walter Pidgeon in Mrs Miniver (1942)**
Married lovers facing wartime with 'True Brit' resistance and stiff upper-lips.

▶**Spencer Tracy and Katharine Hepburn in Keeper of the Flame (1942)**
A Big Combo and Perfect Partners all rolled into one.
Photographer: C. S. Bull

Annette Funicello and Frankie Avalon in Beach Party (1963)
There's a whole lotta barbecue-ing going on: sun, sand and squeaky-clean teens in swimsuits.

Doris Day and Rock Hudson in Lover Come Back (1961)
Untainted love – freckle-faced wholesomeness meets the all-American hunk.

John Wayne and Maureen O'Hara in McLintock! (1963)
The Duke and his Duchess wallowing in the mud of the old West.

▶**Donald Sutherland and Jane Fonda in Klute (1971)**
The detective and the call-girl, screen lovers who are also social misfits. Sutherland and Fonda would team up again, two years later, in *Steelyard Blues*.

Masayuki Mori and Machiko Kyo in Ugetsu Monogatari (1953)
A Japanese screen team familiar to Western audiences through such films as this, Kenji Mizoguchi's
tale of a humble potter (Mori) who falls in love with a beautiful ghost (Kyo).

stars, such as Lucille Ball or Loretta Young, who had never quite made it into the top ranks.

Nevertheless a few screen teams *did* emerge. Married love was celebrated in wholesome style by peachy-clean, freckle-faced Doris Day and her partners, Gable, Grant and, most famously, Rock Hudson in *Pillow Talk* (1959), *Lover Come Back* (1961) and *Send Me No Flowers* (1964). Frankie Avalon and Annette Funicello became the un-crowned king and queen of the teen exploitation market in surf 'n' sand romps such as *Muscle Beach Party* (1964) and *Beach Blanket Bingo* (1965). ('It's for morons!' *The Times* declared, rather churlishly.) Over 20 years later Avalon and Funicello would return to the haunts of their youth in *Back to the Beach* (1987), only this time they would be playing parents, with teen offspring of their own.

Sophia Loren and Marcello Mastroianni got together in a number of Italian sex comedies, which, despite Italy's reputation as a bastion of macho culture, were generally more sophisticated and less misogynous than their Holly-wood counterparts. Mastroianni's screen performances in films such as *Divorzio all'Italiana/Divorce Italian-Style* (1961) had somehow saddled him with the image of the archetypal Latin Lover although, ironically, he usually played weak men, wavering more or less impotently between the demands of wife and mistress. In one of the trio of tales in *Ieri Oggi e Domani/Yesterday Today and Tomorrow* (1963), Loren demands that he keep making her pregnant so she can avoid a prison sentence, and, as his mistress in *Matrimonio all'Italiana/Marriage Italian-Style*

(1964), she resorts to subterfuges such as pretending to be on her death-bed to trick her lover into marriage.

Of course, box-office hits still yielded sequels, although, in the Seventies, *Son of . . .* and *The Return of . . .* tended to be replaced by the appropriate roman numeral after the original title. But these follow-ups were rarely based upon the proven appeal of a particular character, let alone a particular screen partnership. More often, it was a straightforward recycling of the original concept: killer shark, psychopathic killer, killer commando or whatever, backed up by a fresh supporting cast of disposable cannon fodder. Filmstars were canny and powerful enough to demand more money after appearing in a smash hit, and spiralling costs prohibited the development of successful screen combos. (Sylvester Stallone, in *Rocky* (1976) and its sequels, had a romantic pairing of sorts with Talia Shire, but it was hardly the selling-point of the series.)

In the Eighties, a hit film such as *Romancing the Stone* (1984) could demonstrate enough box-office clout to reunite its stars, Kathleen Turner and Michael Douglas, for a second outing, *Jewel of the Nile* (1985). *Heartburn* (1986), the film version of Nora Ephron's *roman à clef*, didn't break any box-office records, but the teaming of Jack Nicholson and Meryl Streep was considered strong enough stuff for the pair to be cast together again in the drunken hobo drama *Ironweed* (1987), adapted from William Kennedy's novel. Such reteamings, however, are the exception rather than the rule today; a different co-star on every outing is the norm.

Sophia Loren and Marcello Mastroianni in Matrimonio all' Italiana/Marriage Italian-Style (1964)
A European earth mother pitting her wits against a Latin lover in Vittorio De Sica's Italian sex comedy.

▲Robert De Niro and Meryl Streep in Falling in Love (1984)

Bankable faces in a brief encounter which didn't exactly set the box-office on fire.

▶Michael Douglas and Kathleen Turner in Romancing the Stone (1984)

A couple of comic adventurers who would reprise their relationship in the sequel, *Jewel of the Nile* (1985).
Photographer: Aaron Rapoport

PRIVATE LIVES

REAL-LIFE LOVERS

Life, as we all know, has a tendency to imitate art, and vice versa. This is especially true of the movies, which specialize in the representation of reality as though it were reality itself. With all the kissing and cuddling that goes on, you can hardly blame the audience for occasionally wondering where the acting stops and the real feelings begin, and publicists have never been above a spot of gossipmongery in order to pique the public's curiosity about the stars' real relationships. The famous 'horizontal' love scene in *Flesh and the Devil* (1927) gained an extra fizz when the studio leaked news that Greta Garbo and John Gilbert were lovers offscreen as well as on. Their next film, an adaptation of *Anna Karenina*, was called simply *Love* (1927); 'John Gilbert and Greta Garbo in *Love* . . . What more could be said about a picture?' as the publicists so accurately put it.

When the simulation of passion requires that real reserves of emotion be tapped, is it any wonder that so many actors and actresses cross the line between pretence and reality and actually fall for their co-stars? Film-making is a collaborative art, one that induces a hothouse atmosphere of enforced intimacy. It can create a network of intense family feeling that usually unravels when the shooting wraps and cast and crew go their separate ways. But sometimes, the spark that is kindled in front of the cameras is fanned into a flame that outlasts the filming.

When Lauren Bacall made her first entrance in *To Have and Have Not* (1944) and demanded 'Anybody got a match?', it must have seemed a foregone conclusion, even to contemporary audiences, that Humphrey Bogart would be willing to supply the goods in more ways than one, onscreen *and* off. This was a dame and a half, one who would give as good as she got and who wasn't content to sit on the sidelines and bat her eyelashes while her co-star got all the best quips. In real life, Bogart's third marriage was already on the rocks, but it was to take another year before he could obtain a divorce and wed Bacall. Despite the 25-year gap between their ages, their marriage turned out to be remarkably successful by Hollywood standards, producing two children and lasting until Bogart's death in 1957. The couple's rapport, showcased in four

Spencer Tracy and Katharine Hepburn in Without Love (1945)
Tracy and Hepburn were at their best when trading wisecracks, but this film, in which a reporter uncovers the unsavoury side of a dead hero's character, was a joke-free drama. It was also the only one of their outings together in which Hepburn dies on screen.

Humphrey Bogart and Lauren Bacall in The Big Sleep (1946)
Bogart as Raymond Chandler's private eye Philip Marlowe. He finds time between murder investigations to engage Bacall's feisty rich girl in some saucy verbal sparring, most memorably when she tells him that her love of horseracing 'depends on who is in the saddle'. *Photographer: Longworth*

films, is one of the most electrifying in cinema history.

It is probably no coincidence that two of these movies, *To Have and Have Not* (1944) and *The Big Sleep* (1946) should have been directed by Howard Hawks. His work, though frequently concerned with rugged masculine values and buddy bonding, gave the movies some of their toughest, smartest heroines.

Katharine Hepburn had also done her stint as a Hawksian heroine, albeit a scatter-brained one, opposite Cary Grant in *Bringing Up Baby* (1938). Unorthodox and wilful,

she was a filmstar on her own terms and labelled box-office poison in the Thirties by an unappreciative Hollywood establishment. Hepburn always took centre stage; she was never content to be a mere supporting actress, and when she starred with Spencer Tracy in *Woman of the Year* (1942), the first of many such collaborations, it was as an equal partner, although Tracy would always insist on top-billing. It was a collusion and collision of opposites: her screen persona was waspish, refined and highly strung, whereas his was gruff, phlegmatic and bullshit-free.

▲Dolores Costello and John Barrymore in When a Man Loves (1926)

A silent film adaptation of Abbé Prévost's novel *Manon Lescaut*, starring real-life lovers who later married. Their first film together was *The Sea Beast* (1926), which attempted to work a romantic relationship into the plot of Herman Melville's novel *Moby Dick*.

►Charlie Chaplin and Paulette Goddard in Modern Times (1936)

Chaplin and Goddard also starred together in *The Great Dictator* (1940). They had been secretly married in 1933, when he was 44 and she was 19 years old. *Photographer: Max Munn Autrey*

In real life, it was Hepburn who provided the rock of level-headed support, enduring Tracy's alcoholic binges and melancholic bouts and nursing him through his long illnesses. She was also accommodating enough to put up with the fact that, as a Catholic, he would never divorce his first wife to marry *her*. (Equal partnerships on screen were never quite so equal behind the scenes: Hepburn would sometimes give up work altogether in order to cater to Tracy's needs, while Bogart criticized Bacall for making movies instead of concentrating on their family life.) It is a measure of the public affection for Tracy and Hepburn that both received Academy Award nominations for *Guess Who's Coming to Dinner?* (1967), his last film (she won, he didn't). Dull, stagey and cloyingly sentimental it might have been, but it was nevertheless a reminder of the devoted duo's former glories.

But the presence in a movie of a real-life husband and wife team was not necessarily a guarantee of box-office success, let alone artistic worth. The only film in which Douglas Fairbanks and Mary Pickford – then Hollywood's premier married couple – starred together was Shakespeare's *The Taming of the Shrew* (1929). It turned out to be a disaster, memorable only for the credit 'with additional dialogue by Sam Taylor'. Thirty-seven years later, the roles of Petruchio and Kate were filled by another real-life couple: Elizabeth Taylor and Richard Burton. These two had met and fallen in love during the protracted production of *Cleopatra* (1963), giving rise to such headlines as 'LIZ AND BURTON FROLIC IN ROME'. The film itself turned out to be a tedious turkey. Despite Taylor's Best Actress Oscar for *Who's Afraid of Virginia Woolf?* (1966), another showcase for squabbling partners in which she mussed up her hair and talked dirty, audiences were more interested in the pair's on-and-off offscreen relationship, especially when the majority of their starring vehicles consisted of such forgettable farragos as *Boom!* (1968) and *Hammersmith Is Out* (1972).

Today the question is not so much 'Are they or aren't they?' as 'Are they *really*?' It is difficult to keep track of who's had whom, who's married whom and who's divorced whom. One can almost trace Warren Beatty's private life by running through his filmography: *Shampoo* (1975) came in the Julie Christie period, *Reds* (1981) co-starred Diane Keaton, and the catastrophic flop *Ishtar* (1987)

Continued on page 96

Richard Burton and Elizabeth Taylor in Cleopatra (1963)
Burton and Taylor fell in love on the set of this megabudget turkey, but whatever chemistry there
was between them in real life didn't show up on screen.

Greta Garbo and John Gilbert in Flesh and the Devil (1927)
The real-life romance of the two stars ensured the huge popular success of this film.

Douglas Fairbanks and Mary Pickford in The Taming of the Shrew (1929)
Hollywood's premier married pair bickering their way through a lack-lustre film version of Shakespeare's play. Richard Burton and Elizabeth Taylor played the roles of Petruchio and Kate in Franco Zeffirelli's 1967 version.

Vivien Leigh and Laurence Olivier in 21 Days Together (1940)
One of the real-life lovers' several outings together, made in 1937, but released only after their
marriage. The screenplay was by Graham Greene, from a play by John Galsworthy about three weeks
of romance prior to a man's trial for murder.

featured Isabelle Adjani. Cutie-turned-serious-actress Jessica Lange and laconic tough-guy playwright/actor Sam Shepard appeared together first in *Frances* (1982), a fairly harrowing account of the downfall and subsequent lobotomy of actress Frances Farmer, and later in *Country* (1984), a hard-times-down-on-the-farm drama which is irresistibly reminiscent of their own determinedly unHollywood existence on a rural ranch, well away from the star circuit.

In fact, it is rare for spouses or partners *not* to appear in at least one film together, although they are not always teamed as the romantic couple. While Timothy Hutton declared undying love for Kelly McGillis in *Made in Heaven* (1987), his wife Debra Winger was on hand, lurking on the sidelines dressed as a male angel. Jack Nicholson and Kathleen Turner provided the central romantic interest as a pair of enamoured hitpeople in *Prizzi's Honor* (1985) but it was Nicholson's longtime girlfriend, Anjelica Huston, who walked off with the Best Supporting Actress Oscar for her role as the disgraced Prizzi daughter who gets her man (Nicholson, natch) in the end.

Marriage to a filmstar has its own special frustrations and pitfalls, even when both partners are stars in their own right. Vivien Leigh turned down the secondary role of Isabella in *Wuthering Heights* (1939) because she wanted to play Cathy opposite the Heathcliff of her husband-to-be, Laurence Olivier. (Merle Oberon got the part.) They had already acted together in the British film *Fire Over England* (1936), but, as far as Hollywood was concerned, Leigh was an unknown quantity. Until *Gone With the Wind* (1939), that is. She and Olivier eventually appeared together again in *That Hamilton Woman*/UK: *Lady Hamilton* (1941), but whatever spark there was between them, it failed to light up the screen in this uninspired biopic.

Tony Curtis's studio, Universal, disapproved of his wedding to Janet Leigh in 1951, on the grounds that it would limit his appeal to a growing army of young female fans. The couple made five films together in all, the most memorable being *The Vikings* (1958), a fullblooded peplum pic. But, despite being dubbed 'The Happiest Couple in Hollywood', the pressures of showbiz took their toll. Marital tiffs were blown up out of all proportion by the fan

Continued on page 102

Mel Ferrer and Audrey Hepburn in War and Peace (1956)
Ferrer played Andrei to his real-life wife's Natasha in King Vidor's epic adaptation of Leo Tolstoy's
mammoth book. Henry Fonda played her ultimate love interest, Pierre.

Sharon Tate and Roman Polanski in Dance of the Vampires/The Fearless Vampire Killers or: Pardon Me, But Your Teeth Are in My Neck (1967)
The Polish actor/director in his fullblooded horror-comedy, accompanied by his bride-to-be. Their relationship ended in the most tragic circumstances when she was murdered in 1969 by the followers of Charles Manson.

Charles Bronson and Jill Ireland in Valdez, il Mezzosangue/Valdez, the Halfbreed (1973)
Ireland has made frequent appearances in her husband's films since their marriage in 1968.

magazines. Curtis's career flourished while Leigh's langu-ished in the doldrums, and the relationship drifted onto the rocks after the birth of their second child, who would later make a name for herself as Jamie Lee Curtis.

Simone Signoret's maternal feelings towards little-girl-lost Marilyn Monroe dwindled rapidly when she found that her husband, Yves Montand, was taking the title of the film in which he and Monroe were co-starring – *Let's Make Love* (1960) – rather too literally. Monroe had apparently arrived at the Frenchman's hotel room one night wearing nothing but a mink coat, and, married or not, few men could have resisted such an invitation.

Nowadays, the power of the individual filmstar is stronger than it ever was. Actors with proven box-office records can sometimes initiate their own projects and select their own co-stars. Stars such as Clint Eastwood own production companies and can ensure that partners (Sondra Locke in Eastwood's case) reprise their offscreen roles in front of the camera. Roping in the missus is evidently a favourite pursuit of action stars, though the

quality of the onscreen relationship usually leaves some-thing to be desired. Charles Bronson sometimes takes his wife, Jill Ireland, along for the ride, and Sylvester Stallone gave his then wife Brigitte Nielsen her first shot at the big time in his starring vehicles, *Rocky IV* (1985) and *Cobra* (1985), before she decided to go it alone opposite Eddie Murphy in *Beverly Hills Cop II* (1987).

An actress's offscreen relationships are not restricted to her co-stars, of course. Female stars have often formed romantic liaisons with their directors, but particularly in the wake of the *auteur* theory. This high-faluting approach to criticism was first promoted in the Fifties by the writers of the French film magazine *Cahiers du Cinéma*, who regarded the director as not just a studio workhorse but a creator, with a consistent artistic vision. Now directors could have star quality too. Jean-Luc Godard, who re-shuffled the Hollywood pack of rules for his own film-conscious purposes, has always been as much a celebrity as Anna Karina, his first wife and the star of many of his early films. Godard, posing casually for photographs with three

Continued on page 106

▶Marlene Dietrich in Shanghai Express (1932)
Passion sublimated to aesthetic ends: a result of the relationship between Dietrich and her director, Josef Von Sternberg. Von Sternberg's wife eventually sued the actress for alienation of her husband's affections; Dietrich contested the case, and won. *Photographer: Don English*

Sondra Locke and Clint Eastwood in Any Which Way You Can (1980)
Locke has appeared in many of Eastwood's movies. This one was the sequel to *Every Which Way But Loose* (1978). In both films, she and the rest of the supporting cast play second fiddle to an orang-utan called Clyde.

Julie Christie and Warren Beatty in McCabe and Mrs Miller (1971)
Beatty's affair with Christie was perhaps the most famous of his numerous romantic liaisons. The duo
also appeared together in *Shampoo* (1975) and *Heaven Can Wait* (1978).

Irving G. Thalberg and Norma Shearer (1927)
Thalberg, known as 'The Boy Wonder', was head of production at MGM when he married Shearer,
one of the studio's stars, on 29 September 1927. The love-match did no harm at all to Shearer's
career.

days' stubble or a French cigarette hanging from his lips, also helped rewrite the rules of glamour: the director as superstar, European style.

Sometimes the collaboration between star and director is purely artistic, though the relationship will still bear the evidence of sexual obsession. Josef Von Sternberg's loving presentation of his protégée, Marlene Dietrich, was supremely erotic in its emphasis on shadow and texture. She was a half-glimpsed image of seduction, swathed in mystery and promise; an illusion created by lighting, camera placement, editing, costume and set design, all calculated to display her in the most flattering way possible.

Producers too could exercise a Svengalian influence over their protégés' careers, or at least ensure that they had first pick of the plum roles: being married to one of MGM's head honchos, Irving G. Thalberg, never did Norma Shearer any harm. Jennifer Jones was carefully

guided and groomed by producer David O. Selznick who she eventually married. (King Vidor, who directed Jones in the ludicrously steamy *Duel in the Sun* (1946), joked that he could actually hear Selznick's heavy breathing on parts of the soundtrack.) Another Hollywood producer, Darryl F. Zanuck, showed rather less discrimination in his choice of protégée. His attempts to promote a succession of lady-friends (Bella Darvi, Juliette Greco, Irina Demick and Genevieve Gilles) in their own starring vehicles met with stony public indifference. A rare example of the sex roles being reversed is that of Alan Ladd, whose career was guided by his wife and agent, Sue Carol.

The career and reputation of the protégée will sometimes outstrip that of the promoter. Roger Vadim, no great shakes as a director, nevertheless displayed an astounding talent for promoting the charms of young actresses such as Brigitte Bardot, Catherine Deneuve and

Brigitte Bardot and Jean-Louis Trintignant in Et... Dieu Créa la Femme/And God Created Woman (1956)
Love and lust à la St. Tropez. Director Roger Vadim remade his most famous film in 1988, with Rebecca De Mornay in the Bardot role.

Jane Fonda. All three women went on to do their most memorable work for other directors. Vadim's first film, *Et ... Dieu Créa la Femme/And ... God Created Woman* (1956) remains his most famous: unveiling Bardot to a goggle-eyed public, which at that time was unaccustomed to having its sex symbols presented in the raw, enjoying sex in a seemingly unabashed and unrepentant manner.

In 1949, Ingrid Bergman shocked the Western world when she abandoned her husband and young daughter to elope with Italian director Roberto Rossellini, compounding this 'sin' by bearing him a child out of wedlock. Americans, who applauded such all-conquering passion when they saw it on the cinema screen, proved unable to countenance the Real Thing. She was pilloried by the press and denounced in the US Senate as 'Hollywood's Apostle of Degradation'. It was not so much that such behaviour was unheard of in Hollywood; it was just that this was *Ingrid Bergman*, an actress who had received Oscar nominations for her portrayal of a nun, in *The Bells of St Mary's* (1949), and of a saint in *Joan of Arc* (1948), an actress whom studio publicity had always promoted as the image of scrubbed saintliness – rumour had it that she didn't even wear lipstick offscreen. She and Rossellini eventually married, and he directed her in a number of films including *Stromboli* (1949) and *Viaggio in Italia/Strangers* (1953), both of which were gloomy studies of troubled marriages. It was not until 1956 that Hollywood signalled its forgiveness by presenting Bergman with an Oscar for her role as *Anastasia*.

Orson Welles's marriage to Rita Hayworth was in tatters when he insisted that she have her long red hair (her trademark) shorn and dyed blonde for her role as *The Lady From Shanghai* (1948), one of the most predatory, heartless *femmes fatales* in movie history. Welles, besides being her co-star, was also writer and director of this flawed masterpiece, and the film is virtually a record of his infatuation, frustration and ultimate impotence when confronted by the real person beneath the façade of one of the screen's greatest sex symbols.

Among Hollywood's most successful marriages is that of Paul Newman and Joanne Woodward, who have co-starred on a number of occasions; the last was *The Drowning Pool*

◄Paul Newman and Joanne Woodward in The Long Hot Summer (1958)
Their first film together, based on short stories by William Faulkner. Joanne Woodward seems to specialize in the type of 'Deep South' woman she plays here.

►Orson Welles and Rita Hayworth in The Lady From Shanghai (1948)
Welles and Hayworth were already well on their way to divorce by the time this film was released. *Photographer: Cronenweth*

(1976), an adaptation of one of Ross MacDonald's Californian crime novels. Somehow they never registered as a Great Screen Team, perhaps because their acting styles are so disparate: one can never forget that Woodward, though talented, is an *actress* giving a *performance*, while Newman, like the best screen stars, has the ability to *exist* in his roles without apparent effort. He has, incidentally, directed his wife in several films, including *Rachel, Rachel* (1968), about an inhibited schoolteacher, and *The Glass Menagerie* (1987), in which she played Tennessee Williams's faded Southern-belle matriarch.

John Cassavetes and Gena Rowlands are something like an arthouse version of Newman and Woodward. Although they appeared together in *Opening Night* (1978) and (as brother and sister) in *Love Streams* (1984), it is more usual

to find Rowlands going solo in films directed by her husband, most memorably *Gloria* (1980), in which she played an ex-moll who takes on the mob in order to protect a small boy.

Woody Allen's leading ladies are nearly always his real-life paramours. His wife Louise Lasser appeared with him in *Bananas* (1971), Diane Keaton in a number of films including *Annie Hall* (1977) (a semi-autobiographical film supposedly inspired by their relationship), and Mia Farrow revealed herself to be an actress of hitherto unsuspected range in *Broadway Danny Rose* (1984), *Hannah and Her Sisters* (1986) and *September* (1988).

Though Allen's nasal whining and intellectual name-dropping can occasionally be off-putting, he is one of the few contemporary film-makers who have attempted to

deal seriously with love and sex, albeit with some humour. His male leads, often played by himself, are neurotic, self-deprecating, sexually-inadequate individuals and his comedy follows in the tradition of Jewish New Yorkers such as S. J. Perelman, plus a touch of arthouse *angst*.

His films, while largely concerned with romantic relationships, are realistic enough to allow that love is not the overwhelming, lifelong passion so often presented in Hollywood movies; nevertheless he frequently pays homage to the Hollywood tradition and the way it enables ordinary people to transcend humdrum reality, as in *The Purple Rose of Cairo* (1985). Allen's lovers meet, argue and drift apart, accepting that people are changed by time and circumstance. They are not real life, but they're as close to reality as we're likely to get on the big screen.

◄**John Cassavetes and Gena Rowlands in Love Streams (1984)**
Cassavetes often directed his wife in heavy-duty emotional dramas and sometimes appeared on screen with her, too.

▲ **Gérard Depardieu and Fanny Ardant in La Femme d'a Côté/The Woman Next Door (1981)**
Ardant's offscreen lover was her director, François Truffaut. She bore his child shortly after his death from cancer in 1984.

►**Diane Keaton and Woody Allen in Manhattan (1979)**
Nervous love in New York City. Keaton was a regular fixture in Allen's middle period (between Louise Lasser and Mia Farrow) and popped up in a cameo role in his more recent *Radio Days* (1987).

Sean Penn and Madonna in Shanghai Surprise (1986)
Intense, brawling brat-packer and top pop superstar: real-life spouses but lacking the essential spark
on screen. This film flopped, and deservedly so.

Sam Shepard and Jessica Lange in Country (1984)
Taciturn masculinity meets starlet-turned-serious-actress – a perfect match.

LOVE HAS MANY FACES

There have been screen teams catering for all tastes. But, whether comic or tragic, singing or dancing, their appeal was always based on the notion of the couple as a fundamental of Western society. Of all the romantic relationships ever depicted on screen, there are only a few which did not draw from a small fund of familiar themes.

There was the lighter side of love, where romantic love conquered all: poverty, separation, combat duty, amnesia, physical disability. It bridged the gap between social classes, matched compatibles and united opposites. Whatever trials were faced, however many traumas were suffered, the audience could bank on an all-forgiving finale when misunderstandings were cleared up as the pair looked forward to a long and contented life (or occasionally afterlife) together. Films which dwelt on love's darker manifestations often ended in tears. Lust, infidelity, jealousy and obsession led to madness, murder and death. Life's infinite possibilities were stripped down to a handful of outlines in which audiences could recognize stock situations and characters and even, in many cases, predict the outcome.

ROMANCE

Films such as *Gone With the Wind* (1939) are lush romances in which the lovers never stop to question the meaning of love itself, but accept it as an uncontrollable force of nature that governs their very existence. These Screen Lovers presuppose that there is one perfect partner lying in wait for each of them. They may get sidetracked, however, by mistaken impressions or the lure of wealth and position. We, the audience, are usually several steps ahead on such occasions. We can easily distinguish true love (Scarlett's love for Rhett) from false love (her infatuation with Ashley). And we *know* that the heroine will eventually see the error of her ways and transfer her affections to Mr Right before the final credits (even if, like Rhett Butler, he says he doesn't give a damn). The same applies to Wendy Hiller in *I Know Where I'm Going* (1945). Headstrong in her

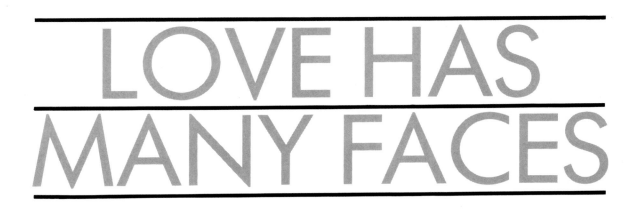

(l to r) Harry Davenport, Clark Gable, Leslie Howard, Vivien Leigh in Gone With the Wind (1939)

Screen Lovers during the Civil War – one of the screen's best-loved romances. *Photographer: Fred Parrish*

determination to marry a wealthy industrial magnate, she refuses to acknowledge her feelings for an impoverished Scottish laird (Roger Livesey) until the very end of the film. The course of true love never did run smooth, and there wouldn't be much of a story if it did. The Astaire and Rogers films alone offer numerous variations on the misunderstanding, the third-party involvement and the will-they-won't-they romance.

Screen Lovers must surmount a veritable obstacle course of barriers lying between them and a happy ending. Sometimes there are possessive relatives or snobbish acquaintances who will frown upon a liaison such as that between widow Jane Wyman and her young bohemian gardener, Rock Hudson, in *All That Heaven Allows* (1955). Occasionally, the loved one will turn out to be a headcase, like Gregory Peck in *Spellbound* (1945). (Fortunately his lover, Ingrid Bergman, just happens to be a psychoanalyst who can help probe his hang-ups.) Sometimes the loved one is hampered by a physical disability, often blindness, which the lover must endure or cure, as does Robert Taylor, playboy-turned-brain-surgeon operating on Irene Dunne in *Magnificent Obsession* (1935), or Rock Hudson applying a scalpel to Jane Wyman in the 1954 remake.

Roger Livesey and Wendy Hiller in I Know Where I'm Going (1945)
The lady gets sidetracked by love in Michael Powell and Emeric Pressburger's romance set against the bleak landscape of the Hebrides.

▲Nino Castelnuovo and Catherine Deneuve in Les Parapluies de Cherbourg/The Umbrellas of Cherbourg (1964)
Screen Lovers set to music. Love found and lost again in Jacques Demy's tear-jerking romance.

◄Rock Hudson and Jane Wyman in All That Heaven Allows (1955)
The widow and the gardener. Love crossing the barriers of class and age in Douglas Sirk's lush melodrama.

Richard Gere and Lisa Eichhorn in Yanks (1979)
The G. I. and the English girl doing their bit for Anglo-American relations during World War Two.

Henry Fonda and Katharine Hepburn in On Golden Pond (1981)
Wrinkly romance: two of Hollywood's old troupers proving that Screen Lovers need not always be in the first flush of youth.

Gregory Peck and Ava Gardner in The Great Sinner (1949)
A costume drama of lovers and gamblers.

GRAND ILLUSION

Romance does not necessarily preclude realism. Some of the most celebrated romantic films are almost cynical examinations of the nature of love and obsession, but that doesn't make them any less affective as love stories. Max Ophüls' *La Ronde* (1950), based on the play by Arthur Schnitzler, is one of the most romantic films ever made, and yet its shimmering circular story is a ruthless dissection of love's illusion and the art of seduction: Screen Lovers going through the motions, unaware that they are part of the eternal dance of desire. The prostitute (Simone Signoret) loves the soldier (Serge Reggiani), who in turn loves the chambermaid (Simone Simon), who loves the young man (Daniel Gélin), who loves the married woman (Danielle Darrieux) . . . And so on until the story comes full circle by taking up with the prostitute again.

Luis Buñuel, in *Cet Obscur Objet du Désir/That Obscure Object of Desire* (1977), underlined the abstract nature of sexual obsession by casting two different actresses, Carole Bouquet and Angela Molina, to illustrate the hard-to-get and easy-going sides of one character, the maid with whom Fernando Rey becomes infatuated. Marlene Dietrich played the same role in another version of the same story, Josef Von Sternberg's *The Devil Is a Woman* (1938). For the man, the object of desire is not a person but a cypher, seeming to exist for the sole purpose of delighting and tormenting him. But characters will often take it upon themselves to play the part of sex object. In George Axelrod's underrated farce, *The Secret Life of an American Wife* (1968), housewife Anne Jackson poses as a prostitute. Unable to go through with the charade, she discovers that her moviestar client, Walter Matthau, is also acting out a role: that of the big-shot celebrity who demonstrates his potency by dallying with prostitutes. Both characters drop their façades and get on famously.

In *The Life and Death of Colonel Blimp* (1943), Deborah Kerr plays all three love objects in the life of Roger Livesey's Blimp, thus illustrating his attraction towards a particular ideal of womanhood. Alfred Hitchcock's *Vertigo* (1958) is a darker study on the same theme; ostensibly a thriller, it is also an examination of the impossibility of romantic fulfilment, with James Stewart moulding Kim Novak into the image of his lost love, who was herself an illusion. Perfect partners exist only in the movies, and even in the movies they sometimes have to be invented.

James Stewart and Kim Novak in Vertigo (1958)
Alfred Hitchcock's haunting tale of the unobtainable object of desire.

1

4

5

8

9

La Ronde (1950)

Max Ophuls' merry-go-round of love: **1**) The Prostitute (Simone Signoret) and the Soldier (Serge Reggiani) **2**) The Soldier and the Chambermaid (Simone Simon) **3**) The Chambermaid and the Young Man (Daniel Gélin) **4**) The Young Man and the Married Woman (Danielle Darrieux) **5**) The Married Woman and her Husband (Fernand Gravey) **6**) The Husband and the Girl (Odette Joyeux) **7**) The Girl and the Poet (Jean-Louis Barrault) **8**) The Poet and Actress (Isa Miranda) **9**) The Actress and the Count (Gérard Philipe) **10**) The merry-go-round comes full circle with the Count and the Prostitute.

▲**Charles Boyer and Hedy Lamarr in Algiers (1938)**
The watered-down Hollywood remake of *Pépé Le Moko* (1937).

►**Warren Beatty and Faye Dunaway in Bonnie and Clyde (1967)**
Arthur Penn's killer couple on the run from the law.

LOVE ON THE RUN

Screen Lovers are often of the fugitive kind, on the run from either villains or cops, and snatching whatever brief moments of passion they can in between dodging bullets or keeping a low profile. Physical danger can sharpen emotions, or it can substitute for sex, as in *Bonnie and Clyde* (1967), where bank robberies give Warren Beatty and Faye Dunaway the kick they cannot achieve in bed. Henry Fonda and Sylvia Sidney in *You Only Live Once* (1937), John Dall and Peggy Cummins in *Gun Crazy* (1948), Farley Granger and Cathy O'Donnell in *They Live By Night* (1949) and Keith Carradine and Shelley Duvall in its remake *Thieves Like Us* (1974) are further examples of the fugitive couple on the wrong side of the law, their love consummated only by death in each other's arms.

In both *Pépé le Moko* (1937) and *Quai des Brumes* (1938), Jean Gabin plays a fugitive hero whose love scenes

with, respectively, Mireille Balin and Michèle Morgan offer futile dreams of escape before nemesis catches up with him. Jean-Paul Belmondo, in *A Bout de Souffle/Breathless* (1960), played a similar character, who is ultimately betrayed to the police by his lover, Jean Seberg.

Innocent fugitives will often find love in the stickiest of situations. Robert Donat gets himself handcuffed to Madeleine Carroll in *The 39 Steps* (1935), incidentally providing the screen with one of its sauciest scenes of stocking removal. Cary Grant hides out in Eva Marie Saint's sleeper compartment in *North by Northwest* (1959) before hanging out with her on the face of Mount Rushmore, and honest cop Harrison Ford takes refuge with Kelly McGillis, a young Amish widow, in *Witness* (1985), until his pursuers force him to disrupt her peaceable religious community with an unholy showdown.

Faye Dunaway and Steve McQueen in The Thomas Crown Affair (1968)
Bank-robbing millionaire versus scantily-clad insurance investigator: high-gloss eroticism played out on the chessboard.

◄**Jean-Paul Belmondo and Jean Seberg in A Bout de Souffle/Breathless (1960)**
The French gangster and the American girl: Jean-Luc Godard's New Wave homage to Monogram Pictures.

▲Sylvia Sydney and Henry Fonda in You Only Live Once (1937)
Fritz Lang's early blueprint for the Bonnie and Clyde story.

◄Cary Grant and Eva Marie Saint in North by Northwest (1959)
The Big Kiss: on the run and into the arms of Hitchcock's requisite ice-cool blonde.

►Kelly McGillis and Harrison Ford in Witness (1985)
A cop finds sanctuary with a young Amish widow in Peter Weir's romantic thriller.

Madeleine Carroll and Robert Donat in The 39 Steps (1935)
Compromising positions: lovers linked together in Alfred's Hitchcock's classic mystery-adventure.

KISS ME DEADLY

Screen Lovers in the *film noir* are a disreputable bunch. The man, usually weak or greedy, is only too willing to fall victim to the wiles of the *femme fatale*, who lures him with a promise of passion into her silken web of intrigue. Fred MacMurray in *Double Indemnity* (1944) is so gobsmacked by Barbara Stanwyck and her slinky ankle chain that he will do anything, even kill, for her. Likewise John Garfield in *The Postman Always Rings Twice* (1946), confronted by Lana Turner in her snugly-fitting shorts, and William Hurt in *Body Heat* (1981), panting after Kathleen Turner.

Escaping from the web is well-nigh impossible, as Robert Mitchum discovers when Jane Greer fouls up his attempts to forge a new life in *Out of the Past*/UK: *Build my Gallows High* (1947). These Screen Lovers are doomed creatures, condemned to pay for their perfidy by incarceration or death. But they are not always confined to the world of shadowy *noir*: Gregory Peck and Jennifer Jones, in *Duel in the Sun* (1946), consummate their passion in the middle of a steamy desert by filling each other with lead at the end of the film; all in lurid Technicolor.

Faye Dunaway and Jack Nicholson in Chinatown (1974)
The private dick and the *femme* who isn't as *fatale* as he thinks she is – Roman Polanski's masterly reworking of the *film noir* themes.

▶**Jane Greer and Robert Mitchum in Out of the Past/UK: Build my Gallows High (1947)**
Mitchum is hopelessly trapped in the silken web of the *femme fatale* in Jacques Tourneur's classic *film noir*. Greer and Mitchum appeared together again in Don Siegel's *The Big Steal* (1949).

140

▲Clara Calamai and Massimo Girotti in Ossessione (1942)
Luchino Visconti's unofficial version of *The Postman Always Rings Twice*, transplanted into Italian neo-realist terms. *Photographer: Civirani*

◀Lana Turner and John Garfield in The Postman Always Rings Twice (1946)
Lust leads to murder in this adaptation of James M. Cain's story, remade in 1981 with Jack Nicholson and Jessica Lange.

▲Kathleen Turner and William Hurt in Body Heat (1981)
The *femme fatale* and her fall-guy. Forties *film noir* melodramatics laced with steamy Eighties sex.

▶Barbara Stanwyck and Fred MacMurray in Double Indemnity (1944)
The *femme fatale* and the insurance salesman in Billy Wilder's *film noir* of the James M. Cain story.

Danielle Darrieux and Charles Boyer in Mayerling (1936)
And it all ends in tears for the crown prince and the commoner. The film was remade in 1969 with
Omar Sharif and Catherine Deneuve.

A KISS BEFORE DYING

These lovers are not necessarily criminals, but no matter: they will be dead by the end of the film. Death, in many cases, can be an extremely practical solution for the scriptwriter. However much Robert Taylor loves Greta Garbo in *Camille* (1936), it is obvious that marriage to a courtesan is not a viable proposition for one of his class. Much more convenient to have her die in his arms. Hollywood always fought shy of mixed marriages, and the stray shell that bumps off William Holden in *Love Is a Many-Splendored Thing* (1955) ensures that his romance with Eurasian Jennifer Jones can go no further than is respectable. Japanese girls fall like flies in the movies: Red Buttons loses Miyoshi Umeki in *Sayonara* (1957), John Wayne is relieved of Eiko Ando in *The Barbarian and the Geisha* (1958) and Dirk Bogarde kisses Yoko Tani goodbye in *The Wind Cannot Read* (1958).

Charles Boyer and Danielle Darrieux see suicide as the only solution in the true story of *Mayerling* (1936): he is a crown prince and she is a commoner. Omar Sharif and Catherine Deneuve endured the same fate in the 1969 remake. Self-immolation is also seen as the only way out for a woman who has strayed from the straight and narrow: Vivien Leigh, ballerina turned prostitute, unable to look Robert Taylor in the face and throwing herself under a truck in *Waterloo Bridge* (1940); Joan Crawford, the married socialite who takes up with lower-class violinist John Garfield before ending it all by walking into the sea in *Humoresque* (1946); Greta Garbo as *Anna Karenina* (1935), kills herself by diving under a train.

More often than not, however, the death of a Screen Lover is merely an unabashed excuse to give the audience what it wants: a sentimental wallow, preferably with a box of Kleenex close at hand. Tragic death rounds the film off nicely, and it also forestalls those nagging doubts about what will happen to the relationship once the final credits have rolled. Ryan O'Neal and Ali MacGraw will never have to contend with infidelity and marital bickering after she has kicked the bucket in *Love Story* (1970). In *One Way Passage* (1932), Kay Francis, dying from heart disease, and William Powell, facing execution for murder, will never have to worry about growing old, gracefully or otherwise.

On the other hand, love can be so powerful that it reunites lovers in an afterlife, like Jeanette MacDonald and Nelson Eddy trilling posthumously in *Maytime* (1937). Or it can enable lovers to reach back from beyond the grave, like Jennifer Jones inspiring painter Joseph Cotten in *Portrait of Jennie* (1948), or, more horrifically, Elizabeth Shepherd haunting Vincent Price in *The Tomb of Ligeia* (1965). Death itself is not immune to love. Walking the earth in human guise, fatal Fredric March falls hopelessly for an ethereal Evelyn Venable in *Death Takes a Holiday* (1934) and Maria Casarès is seriously smitten with poet Jean Marais in *Orphée* (1950).

▲ **Vivien Leigh and Robert Taylor in Waterloo Bridge (1940)**
The ballet dancer and the soldier: love turns to tragedy in a London wartime setting. *Photographer: Willinger*

▶ **James Dean and Natalie Wood in Rebel Without a Cause (1955)**
Untamed youth, Nicholas Ray's story of alienation and tentative teen romance.

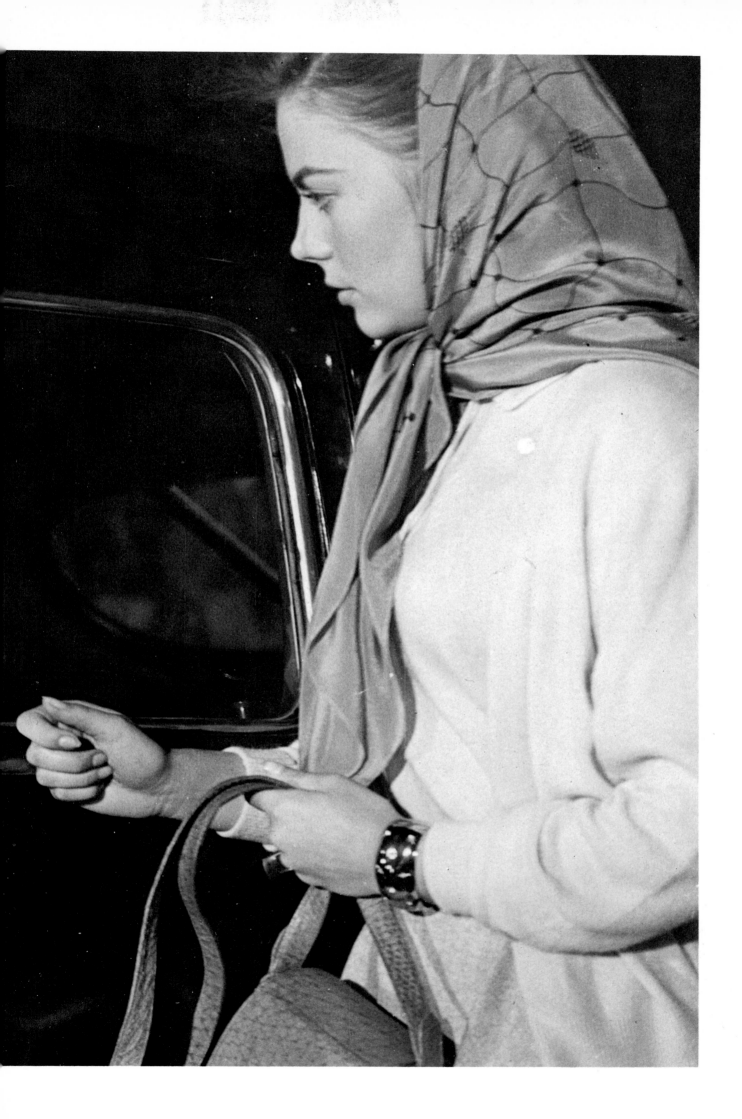

▲Al Pacino and Marthe Keller in Bobby Deerfield (1977)
The racing driver and the terminally-ill Italian girl.

Jeff Bridges and Glenn Close in Jagged Edge (1985) ▲
The publishing magnate and the hotshot lawyer.

◄Ryan O'Neal and Ali MacGraw in Love Story (1970)
Love means never having to grow old gracefully.

▲Joseph Cotten and Jennifer Jones in Portrait of Jennie (1948)
The painter inspired by an ethereal girl.

▶Chlöe Webb and Gary Oldman in Sid and Nancy (1986)
The outer limits of love. The true story of a punk pair overdosing on each other.

THE SACRIFICE

The Screen Lover's sacrifice may end in death, but selfless renunciation can provide an equally poignant conclusion to the affair. Greta Garbo in *Queen Christina* (1933) abdicates from the throne of Sweden for the sake of John Gilbert, her Spanish lover. (But, alas, all in vain; he is killed in a duel on his way to meet her, giving her the opportunity to brood nobly in that famous final shot on the ship's prow.) At the end of *Casablanca* (1942), Humphrey Bogart says: 'I'm no good at being noble', but then goes on to prove that he *is* rather good at it.

In *Brief Encounter* (1945), Celia Johnson and Trevor Howard sacrifice their adulterous romance for the sake of propriety and marital fidelity. The outcome is inevitable; letting passion run its course in this instance would only have resulted in a lifetime of terrible guilt for the pair. Ava Gardner in *Pandora and the Flying Dutchman* (1951) sacrifices herself lock, stock and barrel to save James Mason's soul from an eternity of perdition on the high seas, while in *Intermezzo* (1939) Leslie Howard risks his marriage for the love of his musical protégée.

▲ Celia Johnson and Trevor Howard in Brief Encounter (1945)
Trains that pass in the night: duty and fidelity triumph over extra-marital passion in David Lean's film of Noel Coward's screenplay.

▶ Greta Garbo in Queen Christina (1933)
Love means having to give up the throne of Sweden.

Leslie Howard and Ingrid Bergman in Intermezzo (1939)
Pizzicato on the heartstrings: the violinist and his protogée.

Ava Gardner and James Mason in Pandora and the Flying Dutchman (1950)
The *femme fatale* meets her match in the tall, dark stranger with a past.

►**Ingrid Bergman and Humphrey Bogart in Casablanca (1942)**
A noble sacrifice for the Allied cause.

SMILIN' THROUGH

Not all love stories are tearful affairs with tragic endings. Some of them make us laugh, while offering illuminating insights into human nature and romantic relationships. Comedies deal with infidelity or jealousy as often as do 'serious' films: Jack Lemmon loaning out *The Apartment* (1960) for the extra-marital romps of his business colleagues, and falling for Shirley MacLaine, his boss's latest girlfriend, in the process. Or Rex Harrison in *Unfaithfully Yours* (1948) as the symphony conductor reaching a pathological pitch of jealousy as he imagines Linda Darnell, his very young and innocent wife, to be having an affair. Or Cary Grant as the unscrupulous newspaper editor in *His Girl Friday* (1940), sabotaging the attempts of Rosalind Russell, his ex-wife and star reporter, to settle down with another man.

In the screwball comedy, the woman still has something of the *femme fatale* about her, but instead of luring the man to destruction, she liberates him from his mundane existence in a whirlwind of crazy passion. She is usually one of two extremes: the wealthy (and frequently scatter-brained) society girl, or the wisecracking tart with a heart. Comedies specialize in bringing together ostensibly mismatched couples: Barbara Stanwyck as the conwoman tormenting Henry Fonda's timid ophiologist in *The Lady Eve* (1941) or as the burlesque artiste who runs etymological rings around Gary Cooper's unworldly professor in *Ball of Fire* (1941); Katharine Hepburn's madcap heiress unleashing herself and her pet leopard all over Cary Grant's staid zoologist in *Bringing Up Baby* (1938); Carole Lombard's spoilt little rich girl throwing herself at William Powell's tramp-turned-butler (keeping his wealthy background a secret) in *My Man Godfrey* (1936); Greta Garbo as the stony-faced apparatchik *Ninotchka* (1939), melting beneath the dual spell of Paris and quasi-gigolo Melvyn Douglas; Walter Matthau's sly but penniless playboy in *A New Leaf* (1971), plotting to murder clumsy heiress Elaine May but falling for her instead.

John Barrymore and Carole Lombard in Twentieth Century (1934)
The Broadway producer getting to grips with his actress protégée in Howard Hawks's comedy.

Gunnar Björnstrand and Ulla Jacobsson in Sommarnattens Leende/Smiles of a Summer Night (1955)
Ingmar Bergman's romantic comedy of errors provided the basis for Stephen Sondheim's musical *A Little Night Music*, filmed in 1978 and the inspiration for Woody Allen's *A Midsummer Night's Sex Comedy* (1982).

▶Jean Harlow and Clark Gable in Hold Your Man (1933)
In an era when bedroom scenes were considered somewhat risqué, bathtime offered a perfect excuse to show the leading lady naked. Bubbles were optional.

**Henry Fonda and Barbara Stanwyck in The Lady Eve
(1941)**
The snake-fancier and the conwoman in Preston Sturges's
superb comedy of sexual innuendo.

**►Cary Grant and Ingrid Bergman in Indiscreet
(1958)**
The diplomat and the actress.

**Clark Gable and Claudette Colbert in It Happened
One Night (1934)**
On the road: reporter meets runaway heiress in Frank Capra's
Oscar-winning romantic comedy.

Katharine Hepburn and Cary Grant in Bringing Up Baby (1938)
Letting it all hang out: zany love between an heiress and a zoologist in Howard Hawks's screwball comedy.

Rebecca De Mornay and Tom Cruise in Risky Business (1983)
Boy meets hooker. A lesson in how to turn your house into a brothel when mom and dad are out of town.

PASSION

Sex scenes, of course, are an important component of the romantic film. They need not be explicit for the audience to get the general idea. Directors such as Alfred Hitchcock were fond of suggesting the ultimate consummation by symbolism (which was also a handy way of circumventing censorship). Thus Grace Kelly's capitulation to Cary Grant in *To Catch a Thief* (1955) was suggested with footage of exploding fireworks, and the same actor's enjoyment of conjugal rights with Eva Marie Saint in *North by Northwest* (1959) was signalled by the shot of their train entering a tunnel. But not all Screen Lovers are so coy. Symbolism, especially in recent years, has often been dispensed with in favour of more explicit encounters.

Some Screen Lovers, by boldly going where none have gone before, managed to stretch the limits of what was considered respectable in mainstream cinema: Hedwig Kiesler (later to be renamed Hedy Lamarr) romping nude in *Extase/Ecstasy* (1933), and making love to Albert Mog as the camera closes in on her face, lost in orgasmic rapture; Cary Grant and Ingrid Bergman's record-breaking kiss (accompanied by much nuzzling) in *Notorious* (1946); Burt Lancaster and Deborah Kerr's shameless seashore clinch in *From Here to Eternity* (1953); Jeanne Moreau and Jean-Marc Bory's lingering passion in *Les Amants/The Lovers* (1958), where the camera refused to conform to what was then standard practice and cut discreetly away; Marlon Brando's coupling, stark and tragic in its lack of affection, with Maria Schneider in *Last Tango in Paris* (1972); Tatsuya Fuji and Eiko Matsuda going *all the way* in *Ai No Corrida/In the Realm of the Senses* (1976), their all-consuming affair ending in death and mutilation. These are not necessarily passionate Screen Lovers that we should like to emulate in real-life, but all of them represent landmarks in cinema history for their portrayal of passion.

Anouk Aimée and Jean-Louis Trintignant in Un Homme et une Femme/A Man and a Woman (1966)
All you need is love . . . and lots of kissing.

Albert Mog and Hedy Lamarr in Extase/Ecstasy (1933)
The Czech movie which set pulses racing with its numerous scenes of Lamarr in the altogether.

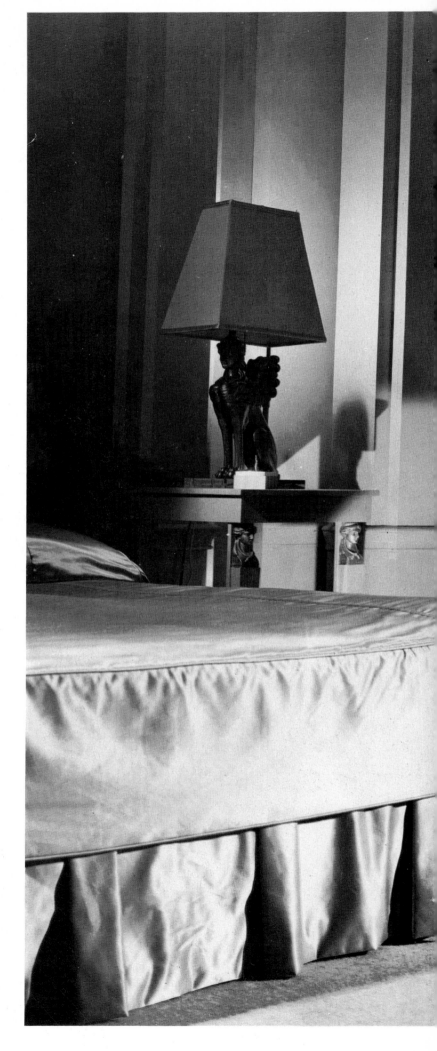

Patricia Neal and Gary Cooper in The Fountainhead (1949)
Architecture and immorality in Ayn Rand's screenplay of her own novel.

LOVE HAS MANY FACES
PASSION

▲Maria Schneider and Marlon Brando in Last Tango in Paris (1972)
Bernardo Bertolucci's study of sex without commitment.

◄Alain Delon and Marianne Faithfull in Girl on a Motorcycle (1968)
When the fur-lined leather catsuit comes off . . .

►Cary Grant and Grace Kelly in To Catch a Thief (1955)
Romance on the French Riviera. The princess of cool with her friendly neighbourhood cat burglar.

Jean-Marc Bory and Jeanne Moreau in Les Amants/The Lovers (1958)
The bored housewife and her young lover. Louis Malle's steamy story of illicit romance ran into censorship difficulties when it was first released.

Burt Lancaster and Deborah Kerr in From Here to Eternity (1953)
Screen Lovers who are not worried about getting their feet wet.

Ellen Barkin and Dennis Quaid in The Big Easy (1987)
Prim femininity meets raffish charm. The romantic encounter which is thinly disguised as a New Orleans cop thriller.

Mel Gibson and Sigourney Weaver in The Year of Living Dangerously (1983)
Hot sex in a hot climate: steamy passion set against the political backdrop of Sukarno's Jakarta.

LOVE HAS MANY FACES

PASSION

**Isabelle Huppert and Gerard Depardieu in Loulou
(1980)**
The little rich girl and her bit of rough.

**Jean-Hughes Anglade and Beatrice Dalle in Betty Blue
(1986)**
The writer and his muse in between bouts of lovemaking.

OUT
OF THE PAST
LITERARY AND HISTORICAL LOVE

Love stories are nothing new. From Adam and Eve onwards, life has been packed full of boy-meets-girl permutations. Film-makers have never been shy about plundering the archives for inspiration, and the origins of many Screen Lovers can be traced back to the classic stories of desire and death played out upon the pages of literature and history.

Popular entertainment has often been regarded with suspicion by the intelligentsia, which prefers its art to be labelled as such and not aimed at a mass audience. It is only since the Fifties (in France) and Sixties (the rest of Western civilization) that movies have been accorded serious critical status as an artform on a par with literature and live theatre. In the Thirties and Forties, moguls such as David O. Selznick were continually seeking to prove that they were artists as well as businessmen, and they believed that what might otherwise have been dismissed as mere melodrama could gain a patina of cultural merit if its source material were, say, Dickens or Tolstoy. Even today, a film which can boast meticulous period detail and a story adapted from an author who provides fodder for English literature classes has gone a long way towards ensuring that critics take it seriously.

But it is no surprise that film-makers return again and again to the classics, whose stories are timeless in their appeal. Shakespeare's *Romeo and Juliet* has provided the blueprint for all subsequent tales of star-crossed lovers and is a perennial favourite with film-makers and stars, many of whom seemed not to care that they were, well, a little *mature* for the roles. Irving G. Thalberg supervised a 1938 production starring his wife, Norma Shearer, and Leslie Howard, aged 32 and 45 respectively when the film was made. Laurence Harvey and Susan Shentall appeared in an uninspired British version (1954), but in 1968 Franco Zeffirelli pulled off something of a coup by casting two teenagers (Olivia Hussey and Leonard Whiting) in the lead roles and appealing to young audiences as much as to lovers of literature. *West Side Story* (1961) added music and dancing and updated the action to New York City in the Fifties, and there have also been a Royal Ballet production, starring Margot Fonteyn and Rudolf Nureyev (1966), and a

Greta Garbo and Robert Taylor in Camille (1936)
Self-sacrifice for the honour of her lover's family. This was Garbo's definitive rendering of the original wilting courtesan.

▲ John Gilbert and Lillian Gish in La Bohème (1926)
Puccini without the tunes: Mimi breathes her last in King
Vidor's silent version of the opera, originally adapted from
Henry Murger's *Scènes de la Vie de Bohème.*

**▶ Olivia Hussey and Leonard Whiting in Romeo and
Juliet (1968)**
Shakespeare for teenagers: Franco Zeffirelli's lavish film
version of the starcrossed lovers gained extra zest from its
youthful, energetic cast.

Sino-Italian variation, *China Girl* (1987). Shakespeare's *The
Taming of the Shrew* and *Macbeth* have provided the
screen with a slew of squabbling and scheming couples,
while any number of vacillating Hamlets and suspicious
Othellos have treated their Ophelias and Desdemonas
disgracefully.

Emily Brontë provided the source book for *Wuthering
Heights* (1939); and it remains the definitive rendering of
amour fou. Directed by William Wyler, the film starred
Laurence Olivier and Merle Oberon as an unforgettable
Heathcliff and Cathy. (Luis Buñuel directed a Mexican
version in 1954.) *Jane Eyre*, by Emily's sister Charlotte, was
filmed in 1944 with Orson Welles and Joan Fontaine (an
example of true love triumphing over blindness) and lent
its storyline to *I Walked With a Zombie* (1943), an
atmospheric chiller produced on the cheap by Val Lewton
and directed by Jacques Tourneur.

Jane Austen's *Pride and Prejudice* gave us a bickering but
witty romantic couple (the Nick and Nora Charles of the
nineteenth century) and was filmed in 1940 with Greer
Garson as Elizabeth and Laurence Olivier as Darcy. *The
Barretts of Wimpole Street*, filmed twice (in 1934 and
1957, by the same director, Sidney Franklin), was history

and literature rolled into a single romantic bundle: one
poet, Robert Browning, successfully wooing another,
Elizabeth Barrett.

French literature has also provided us with its quota of
Screen Lovers. *Madame Bovary*, Gustave Flaubert's classic
tale of a wife who, unable to face reality, allows her
romantic illusions to take over and sacrifices the security of
her bourgeois existence for illicit passion, was filmed in
1934 by Jean Renoir, with Valentine Tessier as Emma
Bovary, and again, in 1949, by Vincente Minnelli, with
Jennifer Jones in the title role. *La Bête humaine/The
Human Beast*, Emile Zola's steamy tale of lust and locomo-
tives, was filmed by Renoir in 1938, with Jean Gabin as the
psychotic train driver whose mistress, played by Simone
Simon, urges him to murder her husband. (Gabin ends up
strangling *her* instead.) The 1954 Hollywood remake,
Human Desire, was directed by Fritz Lang and reunited
Glenn Ford and Gloria Grahame, *The Big Heat*'s cop and
hot coffee combo. The result was something of a bowd-
lerization, with Ford turning out to be a regular
tormented hero.

Stendhal's *Le Rouge et le Noir* and *La Chartreuse de
Parme/The Charterhouse of Parma*, both novels in which

the hero is confronted with a choice between an innocent, unworldly girl and an older, experienced woman, have been filmed, each with Gérard Philipe in the main role; the former in 1954 by Claude Autant-Lara and with Danielle Darrieux as the older woman, and the latter in 1948, directed by Christian-Jacque and co-starring Maria Casarès. Both films, understandably, concentrate on the romantic relationships rather than on the introverted detachment of Stendhal's heroes, since literary adaptations have a tendency to reduce their source material to a simple form.

Victor Hugo's classic Beauty and the Beast tale, *Notre Dame de Paris*, has been filmed three times as *The Hunchback of Notre Dame*, starring Lon Chaney (1923), Charles Laughton (1939) and Anthony Quinn (1956) with Patsy Ruth Miller, Maureen O'Hara and Gina Lollobrigida respectively as gypsy love interest. Alexandre Dumas' *fils* provided the cinema with one of its most popular tragic heroines in *La Dame aux Camélias*, portrayed most memorably by Garbo in George Cukor's 1936 film of *Camille* (although, confusingly, her wilting courtesan was actually

Gary Cooper and Helen Hayes in A Farewell to Arms (1932)
Ernest Hemingway's tale of love under fire given the romantic treament by Frank Borzage. This 'horizontal' scene ran into trouble with the censors.

called Marguerite). Sarah Bernhardt, Theda Bara, Nazimova, Pola Negri and Norma Talmadge are amongst the other stars to have languished in the role. *Camille 2000* (1969) spiked its updated storyline with modish sex and drugs and had its heroine expiring in an oxygen tent, and Zeffirelli gave us Verdi's overtly sumptuous operatic version in *La Traviata* (1982), with Teresa Stratas and Placido Domingo acting *and* singing their socks off on a similarly lavish film set.

Rivalling Emma Bovary for the title of Literature's Most Famous Adulteress is Tolstoy's *Anna Karenina*. Garbo played her twice: first in *Love* (1927), with John Gilbert and a tacked-on happy ending, and again in 1935, with Fredric March. Vivien Leigh followed Garbo under the train in Julien Duvivier's 1948 version. It should be noted here, perhaps, that the cinema follows the example of literature in that illicit, extra-marital passions rarely go unpunished. We are allowed to feel sympathy for the plight of the heroine as she wrestles with her conscience or yearns for passion beyond the restraints of marriage, but

Continued on page 188

Henry Wilcoxon and Claudette Colbert in Cleopatra (1934)
Cecil B. De Mille's epic of ancient Egypt allowed him to indulge to the full his taste for ornate exoticism: history's favourite Screen Lovers surrounded by naked dancing girls and solid-gold trimmings. *Photographer: Ray Jones*

▶**Jean Gabin and Simone Simon in La Bête Humaine/The Human Beast (1938)**
Jean Renoir's version of Emile Zola's steamy novel about a psychopathic train driver and his scheming mistress. Later remade in Hollywood as *Human Desire* (1954) directed by Fritz Lang, with Glenn Ford and Gloria Grahame as the lovers. *Photographer: Sam Levin*

▼**Laurence Olivier and Merle Oberon in Wuthering Heights (1939)**
The Samuel Goldwyn production of Emily Brontë's classic novel of *amour fou*, directed by William Wyler.

▲Laura Del Sol and Antonio Gades in Carmen (1983)
This flamenco version of Mérimée's story, directed by Carlos Saura, blurred the line between real life and performance.

the wages of sin are death, and the woman who cheats on her husband or leads a life of immoral pleasure is marked out for a tragic fate.

Prosper Mérimée gave us another evergreen heroine in *Carmen*, whose story has been filmed at least 18 times, most notably with Theda Bara, Pola Negri and Rita Hayworth in the role. Dorothy Dandridge played her in the all-black *Carmen Jones* (1954), an adaptation of Bizet's opera, and in recent years there has been a veritable glut of hot-blooded señoritas: Jean-Luc Godard's *Prénom; Carmen* (1983), Carlos Saura's flamenco version (1983), Francesco Rosi's film of the opera (1984), plus a triptych of cigarette girls from Peter Brook. Carmen is not so much a *femme fatale* as a saucy slut who gets her come-uppance in time-honoured fashion.

The Bible is not perhaps the most obvious source of Screen Lovers, yet its pages have yielded *Samson and Delilah* (1949), with Hedy Lamarr acting as barber to Victor Mature's muscleman; *David and Bathsheba* (1951), which had Gregory Peck hobnobbing with Susan Hayward in between smiting the Philistines and all those other things that Old Testament kings get up to; *King David* (1985), with Richard Gere and Alice Krige; and Cecil B. De Mille managed to milk love interest from the Book of Exodus with his two versions of *The Ten Commandments* (1923 and 1956), both of which spice their religious message with typically De Millean orgy scenes.

If Eve was the first *femme fatale*, then Cleopatra outstripped her in technique, not to mention wardrobe and make-up opportunities. The Egyptian climate was sup-posedly mild enough to permit an actress to pose in the historical equivalent of a bikini, while her affair with Antony and asp-induced suicide offered plenty of scope for romantic tragedy. Before Theda Bara donned the serpentine brassière in 1917, Cleopatra had already been portrayed at least four times on film. Post-Bara, there were Claudette Colbert abluting in the asses' milk of De Mille's 1934 version; Vivien Leigh in *Caesar and Cleopatra* (1945), courtesy of George Bernard Shaw; Elizabeth Taylor in the 1963 megabudget clinker; Charlton Heston directing himself and Hildegard Neil in Shakespeare's *Antony and Cleopatra* (1973); and even a *Carry on Cleo* (1965), starring Amanda Barrie alongside such comic stalwarts as Sid James and Kenneth Williams.

Historical epics such as Anthony Mann's *El Cid* (1961) temper their heroes' legendary exploits with a human perspective; Charlton Heston must forgo a quiet life with his wife (Sophia Loren) and children in order to die nobly, driving the Moors from Spain with his corpse strapped upright in the saddle. Historical characters who live peaceful, contented lives and die of old age in their beds do not provide suitable material for the screen. No-one has yet made a film about Queen Anne, for example. What is needed is the tug of love between passion and duty, much noble sacrifice and tragic (though often uplifting) death.

In the Eighties, film-makers were keener than ever on literary adaptations. The director/producer team of James Ivory and Ismail Merchant churned out films based on the work of Henry James and E. M. Forster, and hit the box-office jackpot with *A Room With a View* (1985), the slight

Continued on page 194

▶Rita Hayworth in The Loves of Carmen (1948)
Prosper Mérimée's story of the spitfire señorita, filmed many times. Hayworth's Don José was Glenn Ford, who was also her co-star in *Gilda* (1946) and *Affair in Trinidad* (1952). *Photographer: Cronenweth*

**Joan Fontaine, Laurence Olivier and Judith Anderson
in Rebecca (1940)**
The eternal triangle with a twist. One of the angles is dead,
but the housekeeper stands in for her in Alfred Hitchcock's
film of Daphne du Maurier's Gothic romance.

▲Richard Beymer and Natalie Wood in West Side Story (1961)
Romeo and Juliet revisited on the mean streets of New York City; the all-singing, all-dancing update
of Shakespeare's much-filmed story.

▶Charlton Heston and Sophia Loren in El Cid (1961)
Anthony Mann's mediaeval spectacular, in which the Cid forsakes his wife and family in order to die
heroically while driving the Moors from Spain.

▲ Audrey Hepburn and Sean Connery in Robin and Marian (1976)
The return to Sherwood Forest. Menopausal romance in Richard Lester's reworking of mythical characters.

▶ Julian Sands and Helena Bonham Carter in A Room with a View (1985)
E. M. Forster's comedy of English manners, brought to the screen with impeccably good taste by the Merchant-Ivory team.

but charming tale of a young Englishwoman who refuses to acknowledge herself capable of passion. Forster's *A Passage to India* was given the cast-of-thousands David Lean treatment (1984). Such films are often accorded the same reverence as literature, but the emotional relationships within them are usually swamped by an almost pedantic attention to period detail; they are essentially movies for people who don't like movies.

Hollywood, meanwhile, has proved that it can still turn out a prestige item like Sydney Pollack's *Out of Africa* (1984). This combined the elements of literary biopic (the life of Danish author Karen Blixen), travelogue (picturesque Kenyan landscape), and nostalgia-fest (harking back to the days of colonialism), but mostly it was an excuse for a love story in the grand manner, with Meryl Streep nurturing a passion for Robert Redford, improbably cast as her English lover. This heavyweight concoction, despite being lumbered with an excessively mannered performance from Streep succeeded in hitting both the box-office and the Academy Award givers in the right places.

THE
ODD COUPLE
UNUSUAL PAIRINGS

Relationships in the romantic mainstream are usually conducted between Caucasian men and women with regular features, trim figures and an enviable freedom from normal, everyday complaints such as dandruff, eczema, asthma or even the common cold (the illnesses of Screen Lovers are *much* more interesting than that). If they wear spectacles, these are more an indication of academic intellect or spinsterish disposition than an aid to better eyesight. Spectacles are only there to be cast aside when the heroine is transformed by love and emerges, sleek and desirable, from her frumpish shell.

But Screen Lovers are a ubiquitous species. Although their natural habitat lies within the romantic genre and its offshoots, they can also pop up where you least expect them. And in such out-of-the-way places they may not always be pin-up material. They may not even be human. But they love and hate the same as everyone else.

Gaston Leroux's anti-hero, *The Phantom of the Opera*, harbours human desires beneath his hideously scarred face, and furthers the singing career of his female protégée with something of the zeal of a demented Darryl F. Zanuck. He was played by Lon Chaney terrorizing Mary Philbin (1925), followed by Claude Rains spooking Susanna Foster (1943) and Herbert Lom freaking out Heather Sears (1962). William Finlay took the role in Brian De Palma's rock 'n' roll parody *Phantom of the Paradise* (1974), with Jessica Harper as the singer.

David Cronenberg's remake of *The Fly* (1986) is not so much a horror film, despite the gruesome special effects which transform Jeff Goldblum into a monster, as a touching love story that deals with the decay of the flesh and its effect on the romantic relationship between Goldblum's dotty scientist and a journalist, played by Geena Davis.

Films in which monsters or aliens develop relationships with a human being are covert variations on the taboo notion of bestiality. Jean Cocteau's *La Belle et la Bête/Beauty and the Beast* (1946) is the classic fairytale romance between a human heroine and a monster. The beast is so sympathetically portrayed by Jean Marais that when he turns into a traditional prince in frilly

Lon Chaney and Mary Philbin in The Phantom of the Opera (1925)
The man behind the monster mask and his *prima donna*. The first and best of many filmed versions of Gaston Leroux's *Grand Guignol* melodrama.

Fay Wray in King Kong (1933)
Tall, dark stranger seeks petite blonde with powerful lungs for company while fending off
pterodactyls, scaling skyscrapers etc.

Jean Marais and Josette Day in La Belle et la Bête/Beauty and the Beast (1946)
Jean Cocteau's fairytale lovers. Belle with the human suitor who will eventually be transformed into
the princely version of her Beast. *Photographer: G. R. Aldo*

romper-suit and tights it is something of a letdown; any girl with taste would have preferred him fanged and furry, animalistic urges and all. But Beauty and her Beast pop up in a multitude of other incarnations. *King Kong* (1933) manages to retain our affections, even when he's munching on underground passengers or swatting aircraft, because of his bemused, uncomprehending passion for Fay Wray.

Boris Karloff in *Bride of Frankenstein* (1935) offers a poignant portrayal of unrequited love, this time not for a human being but for another monster, the shock-haired Elsa Lanchester. They may have been literally *made* for each other, but alas, that's no guarantee of compatibility. John Carpenter's *Starman* (1984) examines the love between an alien, conveniently assuming temporary human form as Jeff Bridges, and a human Karen Allen, who is left at the end of the film expecting their child. We are given no hint as to which parent the infant will take after, or how the maternity ward will cope. Such are the perils of the mixed marriage.

Dracula has always been the deadliest of paramours, though it took Christopher Lee (1958 onwards) and Frank Langella (1979) to add sex-appeal to Bela Lugosi's sinister but stout interpretation (1931), preying on female victims

who seem only too eager to have their jugulars excavated by tall, dark and handsome strangers. Klaus Kinski, in Werner Herzog's *Nosferatu the Vampyre/Nosferatu: Phantom der Nacht* (1979) is ugly as sin, but manages to communicate something of the unearthly creature's terminal desires when confronted by Isabelle Adjani's noble sacrifice. The vampire, perhaps more than any other screen bogeyman, is redolent with sexual symbolism, and his bite often serves to liberate his victims' libidos from the polite restraints of the stuffy bourgeois household (even if their consequent lack of discretion earns them a stake through the heart).

Paedophilia, not surprisingly, has never been seen as a fit subject for the movies (the Production Code ruled that the sex organs of children were never to be shown, even in the most innocent of contexts) and Graham Greene got himself into legal hot water for daring to suggest that Shirley Temple's appeal was anything other than wholesome. Tennessee Williams's *Baby Doll*, filmed by Elia Kazan in 1956, managed to hedge its bets by casting Carroll Baker as the thumbsucking child-woman, even though the actress was well into her twenties. And Vladimir Nabokov's *Lolita* was brought to the screen by Stanley Kubrick (1962)

Continued on page 203

Elsa Lanchester and Boris Karloff in The Bride of Frankenstein (1935)
Made for each other: James Whale's horror fantasy of science's efforts at matchmaking. Lanchester also played Mary Shelley in the film's prologue.

Isabelle Adjani and Klaus Kinski in Nosferatu, Phantom der Nacht/Nosferatu the Vampyre (1979)
The ultimate love bite, delivered by the 'undead' lover in Werner Herzog's remake of F. W. Murnau's
silent *Nosferatu* (1922).

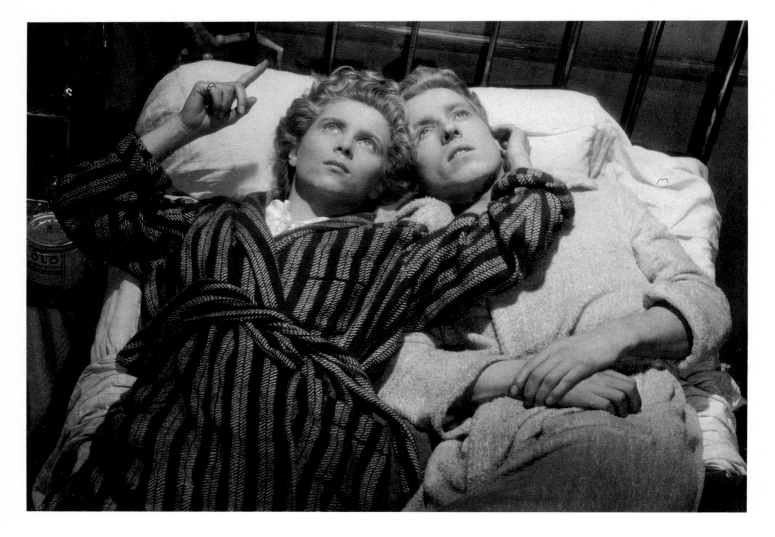

Nicole Stephane and Edouard Dermithe in Les Enfants Terribles/The Strange Ones (1949)
Jean-Pierre Melville's film of the Jean Cocteau story about the obsessive relationship between a
brother and sister.

into the movies. It cropped up on occasions such as James Mason whacking his walking-stick down on Ann Todd's hands in *The Seventh Veil* (1945), or was hinted at in innocent situations which now, with hindsight, seem outrageous: heroines bound tightly to their chairs or heroes administering a good spanking to wilful women.

Alain Robbe-Grillet introduced a spot of bondage in amidst the convoluted narrative trickery of *Trans-Europ-Express* (1967), with Jean-Louis Trintignant tying Marie-France Pisier to the bed. Luis Buñuel, in *Belle de Jour* (1967), depicted the masochistic fantasies of Catherine Deneuve who, unbeknownst to her wealthy husband, works the day shift in a brothel. Barbet Schroeder's *Maîtresse* (1976) exposed the conventional heart that beat beneath the rubber-clad breast of the dominatrix (Bulle Ogier distracted from her trussed-up clientèle by Gérard Depardieu). *Salo – The 120 Days of Sodom* (1975) was Pier Paolo Pasolini's attempt to bring the work of the Marquis de Sade to the screen. But by setting it in the context of Fascist Italy, the director only succeeded in ironing out the book's more bizarre surrealist philosophies into a run-of-the-mill atrocity exhibition, all murder and mutilation.

The only recent example of the Hollywood mainstream addressing itself directly to offbeat desires, $9\frac{1}{2}$ *Weeks* (1986), was a resounding flop. The general consensus was that it didn't go far enough; its sex scenes, swamped by tricksy backlighting, soft focus and designer lingerie, presented no more than a yuppie idea of a kinky relationship, with Kim Basinger and Mickey Rourke as the clothes horses. Sadomasochism was far more successfully realized in David Lynch's *Blue Velvet* (1986), which managed to delve into the dark heart of sex and its links to violence, with Isabella Rossellini, the daughter of Ingrid Bergman and Roberto Rossellini, allowing Dennis Hopper to do unspeakable (but not unfilmable) things to her.

As always, mainstream movie-makers play it safe, trying to avoid any kind of perversion that might get them into trouble with the censors or, even worse, harm their box-office prospects. Exploration of love's murkier territories is left to the European *auteurs*, maverick directors such as David Lynch, or horror maestros like David Cronenberg. It is with them that Screen Lovers can continue to reveal their darker nature.

Karen Allen and Jeff Bridges in Starman (1984)
The widow and the alien who assumes the form of her dead
husband – *E.T.* with added love scenes.

▶**James Mason and Sue Lyon's legs in Lolita (1962)**
The professor and the nymphet: Stanley Kubrick's film of
Vladimir Nabokov's screenplay, adapted from his own novel.

with sixteen-year-old Sue Lyon as a decidedly mature nymphet, lusted after by an older man; James Mason as Humbert Humbert.

In the Seventies, there were no such qualms about the exploitation of minors. Twelve-year-old Jodie Foster played the hooker and object of Robert De Niro's infatuation in *Taxi Driver* (1976) and Brooke Shields wasn't much older when she played a Storyville prostitute loved by photographer Keith Carradine in Louis Malle's *Pretty Baby* (1978). Malle had previously dealt with the subject of incest between mother and son in *Le Souffle au Coeur/Dearest Love* (1971), a theme which was revisited by Bernardo Bertolucci in *La Luna* (1978), in which Jill Clayburgh's diva goes to bed with her drug-addicted son, Matthew Barry. Intimations of incest also figured in Jean-Pierre Melville's *Les Enfants Terribles/The Strange Ones* (1950), adapted from the book by Jean Cocteau; brother and sister, played by Edouard Dermit and the marvellous Nicole Stéphane, are besotted with each other.

Although romantic pictures often deal with extremes of emotional endurance and although many Screen Lovers allow themselves to be treated in a manner bordering on the perverse, unabashed sadomasochism made a late entry

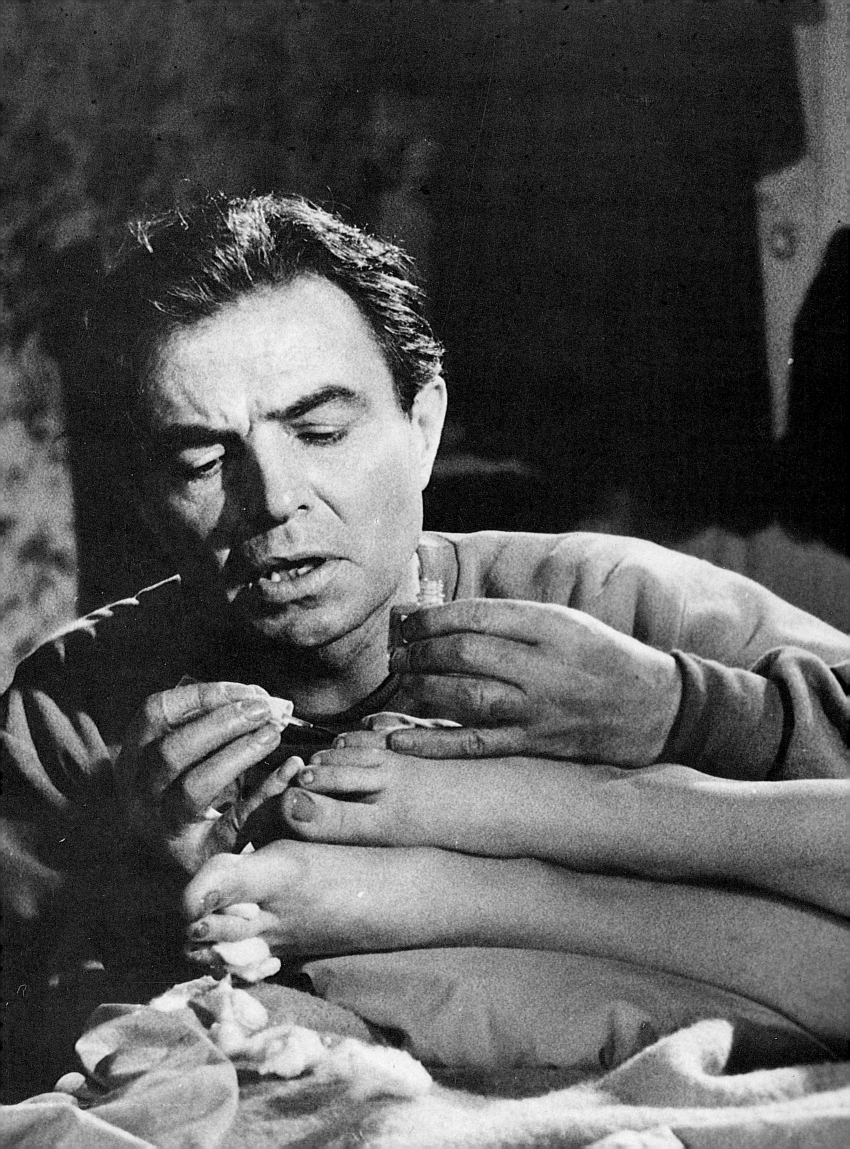

**▲Tatsuya Fuji and Eiko Matsuda in Ai No Corrida/
In the Realm of the Senses (1976)**
Love ends in death and mutilation in Nagisa Oshima's
provocative study of sexual obsession.

**◄Kyle MacLachlan and Isabella Rossellini in Blue
Velvet (1986)**
The festering underbelly of smalltown America. David Lynch's
bizarre peek into the darker side of sexuality.

INDEX

INDEX